A FAN TO A MAN

BY JOSH GEORGE

DORRANCE
PUBLISHING CO
EST. 1920
PITTSBURGH, PENNSYLVANIA 15238

Dorrance Publishing Co
585 Alpha Drive
Pittsburgh, PA 15238
Visit our website at *www.dorrancebookstore.com*

ISBN: 979-8-8872-9086-7
eISBN: 979-8-8872-9586-2

PROLOGUE

The prologue of Josh George's autobiography *A Fan to a Man*.

As the three of us were pacing around, we just wanted to graduate. Then several thoughts danced in our minds. Had we left an impact? Had we done enough? What was the future to be like? How long was this graduation really going to last? Was there time for one last prank? It was questions like these that set in the mind of a college student. In fact, many times throughout a career these thoughts hit.

I was standing there, about to go across the stage, about to go into the gym. The gym that people had called my gym. People thought of this place as my place. I love that place. As I walked into the gym, I was in between two men. Two men who had a major impact on my life. I felt a *phileo* for these two men. *Phileo* is a Greek word that means love, but not like we think of as American love. The definition of *phileo* love is a love that is compassionate, affectionate, fondness, the love that brothers should share. As for me and these two men, we were very much brothers in Christ, as well as brothers in our love for sports.

I had been a leader; one that had helped to change the perception of the school's athletic programs. I could not really be done, could I? That is the question I was asking myself. Ecclesiastes 3 states that there is a time for everything. So that must mean there is a time to graduate college. This was my time to graduate. I walked into that gym, and I realized it really was my time to graduate. I turned to the man behind me and made a bet not long before taking my seat. The man I made the bet with had made me a part of the group, so I made the bet knowing that one day we would indeed have to see each other once more. It was not long until a man took the stage to give the commencement speech. He started talking about all the good deeds we had done and would go on to do, but as he started to close, he stated a quote. This quote is a major theme in a college career. As he started into the quote, me and the man on my right started saying it also. We said, "You cannot connect the dots looking forward. You can only connect the dots looking backwards, so you have to trust that the dots will somehow connect in your future. You have to trust in something: your gut, destiny, life, whatever. Because that will give you the courage to follow your heart even when it leads you off the well-worn path." These words would give me the confidence to persevere no matter what, and the point of this book is to help you find ways to persevere no matter what.

This book will also teach ways of making friends who are people to share God's love with. With that, this book will be a miraculous story of triumph, failure, and change. Change of perception of an athletic program, change in a life, and change on a college campus. It will also answer the question of how or do fans impact college sports. Other things to note, I won the bet; I walked across the stage and got my diploma. There were photos taken in the entrance to the gym. These photos were taken in front of a glass case that displayed my award. The award in my namesake, the Josh George Award. It is to be given out to the best fan of SNU athletics. I had started something great. I was pleased, but I did not know that it would end this way, nor did I ever think of getting honored like this. So, all in all, this is my story: the story of the Josh George Award. A story of how to make it in college.

CHAPTER ONE: GOD'S PATH

"My feet have closely followed God's steps; I have kept to God's way without turning aside."- Job 23:11

I was not totally a Job, but if God made a path for me, I would usually take it, and God clearly wanted me to go to SNU. I have a very loving family. I grew up living with my younger brother Jeremy George, my mother Rhonda George, and my father John M. George. It was a good life. Before I even had reached high school, I had been to lots of Sooner sporting events, as I had started attending Sooner sporting events when I was only three months old. We attended First Presbyterian Church of Norman. When I was growing up, three things were true. First, we go to church on Sundays; next, we watch as many OU (The University of Oklahoma) sporting events that we can. Third, we are there for each other. That was kind of my family's motto.

If I haven't talked about the fact that I was a sports fan, then I must make such an important statement in which its value cannot be understated. I love sports! Growing up, I would often yell at the TV.

This included trying to hug the TV after watching OU beat FSU in the 2000 National Title game. I spent the 2000 National Title game with my grandparents because my parents went to the game in Miami. I remember the moment that they got back. Like most parents, the first thing that they asked was: How were they? Then my Grandaddy answered them… "Josh loves football, doesn't he?"

Then my mom asked, "How could you tell?"

"He reenacted every play either with a mini football or with some action figures that he brought up from the basement."

I was very emotional when it came to my team, and these emotions were not always positive. In 2003 I went to New Orleans, and I stayed with one of my cousins. I remember trying to break the TV after that game. I got in loads of trouble. I'll save you the particulars.

Another thing that is important to know about me is that I'm kind of a hopeless romantic. When I was a sophomore in high school, I asked my girlfriend at the time to a semiformal dance by pulling a chopstick out of my back pocket, then handing it to her, and written on it in big dark letters was, "Will you be my other chopstick to the dance?" I wanted to be that fun guy that could surprise and flatter a girl; this is just part of who I am.

I did not plan on going to SNU. I wanted to go to OU until I was a senior in high school. Then I was offered a contract to play AA baseball with the Mississippi Braves, but only if I went undrafted in the 2013 MLB draft. It was an okay deal, but my mom was insistent that I went to college. The thing was, my grades were not good enough to get me into OU even if the baseball team had offered me a chance to walk-on. My only scholarship offer going into my senior year was from the Air Force Academy in Colorado Springs.

A combination of things led to me finding SNU. I hurt my knee my senior year of high school. The baseball coach stopped playing me. The Braves, OU, and Air Force withdrew their offers. Also, at this time I was not the world's greatest student. By this I mean my GPA was not good: it was all of 2.5; my ACT was 21. (Not great.) I applied to SNU and UCO, hoping one would want me. I was okay with going to UCO. I only applied to SNU because there was a rumor that they accepted everyone.

I did a campus visit to both campuses. When I was on the SNU campus, I felt strangely at home. I met a man named Kyle Boone. He would be my recruiter. He had played basketball at SNU and thought it was the greatest. I enjoyed getting recruited by Kyle. At the end of my high school senior year, I became an Eagle Scout; with this came a major scholarship which included but was not limited to my room and board. He also sent a hat and many T-shirts. Things were opening up. The money was in place, I enjoyed being on campus, and Kyle talked to me about walking on as a baseball player.

At this point, I had decided to go to SNU. I had a great interview with Kyle. On my visit everyone was so good to me the choice was obvious. One of the things in this world that I loved was college football. SNU was 0-11 in my senior year of high school and had won two of their last twenty-four games. Little did I know, because if I had known that I might not have gone to SNU. The majority of SNUs athletic teams had finished with a losing record. For some reason, I did not look much into the sports programs at this time.

It was time to pray. Something important to know that everyone should practice. Prayer is important, and a person should be in constant prayer with God. For major events, it is very important to pray to ask God is this the correct move. So, I prayed with my mother, father, and brother. As the SNU stuff kept rolling in, and I had a dorm number, I was almost committed, but it was that night I got a call from a UCO recruiter. Her name was Jenny; she sounded great. I asked her if she would pray with me about where I should go. She then stated, "I'm not the most religious person in the world anyway."

I still wanted to pray with someone that I was not related with. I asked a good friend that I met in the first grade when we were six years old. His name was Colin Pasque. I asked him to pray for me about where we should go to college. He said, "I will pray for you, but I already know where I want to go."

I asked him, "So where are you going to college?"

He responded, "To SNU in Bethany, Oklahoma." My mouth dropped six feet from my face to the floor. He asked if I was okay. I then told him that I was going to SNU; I knew at that point it was definitely the place God wanted me to go. Believe me, nothing I had done was as cool as the things that I would do in college.

CHAPTER TWO: THE PERFECT FAN

"For we live by faith, not by sight."- 2 Corinthians 5:7

Before I get into my college stories, it is important to know that I was called by God to be the perfect fan for SNU. The perfect fan is always supporting the team and always paying attention to the game. Games are not necessarily a social event, and everything that happens at a game needs to help the team win. The perfect fan is like the twelfth man at Texas A&M. Games and sports can be very romanticized. It's important to know when to cheer and when not to even make a sound. These teams... These sports can become a part of you. SNU became a part of me, and OU already was a part of me. A fall Saturday has places like Michigan where 112,000 fans roar as one person.

These chants and ideas make a community. This shows itself in many ways for Auburn fans when they see each other. A simple

War Eagle can be the start of a long conversation of two strangers that know nothing about each other than they like the same football team. From 2008–2018, under Nick Saben Alabama's National Merit Scholars increased by 60 percent and tuition increased 110 percent as Alabama became the winningest college football program in this timeframe. Ninety-five percent of the Florida Gators' profit line is owed to some kind of sports program. This just goes to show that any good college needs good athletics. My family was a college sports family, and that is a way that we are relational to others because we know so much about what happens and how important sports are to a college. I took this with me to SNU.

CHAPTER THREE: NSI

"In their hearts, humans plan their course, but the Lord establishes their steps."- Proverbs 16:9.

This could not be more true for me. At this point, I had declared to be a history major, made a class schedule, and thought that I had set my path up well at SNU. The Lord would establish my steps, and it showed during NSI. I had done some talking with Colin Pasque over the summer, yet we had not talked about where we would live, yet both of us ended up living in a dorm called Snowbarger. I was one floor up from Colin. I have quite the affection for the Snowbarger; it was an all-boy dorm. A place with boys in newfound freedom; freedom that was used in unique ways. If you keep reading this book, you will hear many stories that came from living in that dorm, and it all started on move-in day.

The day was Saturday, August sixteenth, 2013, at 8:07 a.m. My family and I had just pulled into the parking lot of Snowbarger. We were in my parents' Chevy Traverse. My car needed some work, and I would drive it up to school next semester. I was thinking about this as well as how long would it take to move all of my stuff up to room 512. Room 512 was my room; college was going to be great.

I didn't have to think any more about that because as I got out of that car, I was swarmed by five people in yellow shirts. They screamed softly at me with so many high energy words! They said things such as "What's your room number? "We can take this stuff up for you, it's our job!" Then one said, "I'm Jeremy. Where's the fridge?" He found it before my dad could even point it out. They were great! I had the answer to the question how long would it take to move all of my stuff up to my room? Seven minutes is how long it took for the yellow army of people to move my stuff up to my room.

My mom found a chair to set down and make suggestions about how the room should be set up. My brother hung up posters; as for me and my dad, we set up the furniture. When we were almost done, there was a knock on the door. We all thought that would be my roommate, but it was the RA (resident advisor). He was great; he had the voice of a coach. He prayed with us and gave me the NSI schedule, told me about the other events happening on campus that day. He was the kind of guy that could talk someone into running through a brick wall.

When we were done setting up the room it was barely ten o'clock. It was time to finish the enrollment process. I found out that my college fund had sent more money than necessary, and I would be getting a check in September. Then it was time to walk the main campus finding my classes. It didn't take long before I glanced at some rows of tents. That meant before I found the location for the rest of my classes, we had to see what was going on with those tents. The tents were clubs set up to recruit freshmen. Though they all seemed cool; the only one that I ended up signing up for was to get emails of when the intramural sports were.

The day went on, I got to meet my roommate. After saying hi to me that day he would go on to say no more than five words to me the rest of the semester. When I think of him, the best way to describe him is to say he was lots like "Kenny," Axal's roommate in the TV show *The Middle*. Some advice is to know that going into college, you're going to meet lots of personalities; find the ones that you can jive with and try to be open. Nevertheless, that night came, and with it the ceremony for becoming an official college student on the campus of SNU. During the ceremony, students met with groups, known as family groups, that became their NSI groups. These groups consisted of freshman, male and female upperclassmen called group leaders, and then a professor. In my group there were seven freshmen. Some people seemed helpful, and others not so much. Some I could jive with, and others not so much. I think it is important to be open and honest in order to find people to jive with.

After introductions, I got the who's new at SNU book and talked to people; it was time for the ceremony. We held candles, talked about the light of God, did something with ivy, said good-bye to our parents, enjoyed the pomp and circumstance of joining SNU as we all had a new home. For some it would last a year or less; for others, it would be more than four.

The next day was crammed packed with events! I participated in more "get to know you" activities than I ever had before. I was tired of all these talks, how-to-survive-college skits, trying to learn the alma mater, and being super busy. I just wanted to relax and enjoy living in my new room. Something of note: even if everything seems new, embracing it can help getting off to a good start in college. Now it was 5:50 that Monday and we had ten minutes to change into something black and meet our group on the Snowbarger lawn for some event called the Siren.

This ended up being a competition that I would love. It was the perfect thing after what seemed like a day that was longer than it should have been. All the freshmen were divided up into four teams. It was the black team, the red team, and the white team. Each team would get points for winning head-to-head events, and the team that won the most events would be crowned that champion. Each event would start when the siren made one loud blast and ended after two short siren blasts. We played games like ultimate frisbee, bocce ball, corn hole, human foosball, and other ridiculously unique, fun games. My team never lost a match, and as a result, we won the event. Though there was no prize, we had bragging rights for the rest of that night, in fact after that night, I never really said anything else about it, but it did help shape me because that loud siren blast would become part of my genetic code and DNA. In some of the moments that I heard it, it put me in the mindset to become SNUs biggest fan.

That was all far off. After coming back to my dorm room from the siren event, I let my mind wander. I thought about things, like my family; I tried to talk to my roommate; and I thought about the girl I met at a church camp last summer. In college, there is lots of time to think, and a lot to think about. An important thing is to know yourself when you need to think alone or with others because good friends always help. She was one of the most beautiful girls I had ever seen. I soon discovered that there was always another girl to meet on campus. With this running through my mind, I looked out the window to see lots of barefoot people migrating to the campus volleyball courts. I had to go down there. So I did, and I really enjoyed myself. I got on a team with some of the people in my family group. We had lots of fun meeting some super great people along the way. As I walked back to my room that night, I got two girls' numbers. I would never text either one of them, but I learned a life and college lesson: do not be afraid to be social.

The next day would have a huge impact on my life. It happened on the morning of August 18, 2013. We were all sent to chapel to listen to a sermon about living a God-centered life. I went down to the altar for the first time in my life after that sermon. It was more like I saw the light once more. I decided then to get into whatever it was that God wanted me to do, and I would do the best I could. I spent the rest of my day thinking about that one moment, but there were more lectures and another day of little free time, yet I had been focused.

The next day we spent all morning doing a service project. We built the foundation for a new home. It was so much fun. I felt God's love the entire time I was doing that project. I got paired with a big football lineman, and we wound up working well together. We had a little conversation. It was from this experience that I learned to be a student of God, one must create and cultivate good things. I was starting to understand Proverbs 16:9. That night we were told once again that we had ten minutes to change into cowboy-looking clothes and meet on Snowbarger lawn. We would get on a bus and go to a two-step/line dance. I had a blast! I danced with eleven girls. I can tell you now Proverbs 16:9 means going with your gut, being active, and participating.

On the last day of NSI, my family group had only eaten breakfast together. After that, our two leaders gave us the rest of the day off to do any business that we needed to do because the next day classes started. I decided to watch a four-hour Civil War movie called *Gettysburg*. In that movie, there is a line delivered by Martin Sheen as Robert E. Lee: "It's all in God's hands now." Lee, of course, made a battle plan that had not worked, yet he trusted in God no matter what. That day I made my battle plan for college. I wrote down three goals that I wanted to accomplish. The first was to graduate. The second was to impact lives on campus the best that I could, and the third was to leave an impact on the campus. Then a bonus goal of that day was to enjoy some college sports as a college student. I wanted to cheer on teams from a student section and rush the field after a big win.

CHAPTER FOUR: A HERO'S REFUSAL

"The word of the Lord came to Jonah son of Amittai: Go to the great city of Nineveh and preach against it because its wickedness has come up before me" Jonah 1:1–4.

Next, I was like that. I was called by God to help make SNU athletics better in any way that I could, but that first semester I missed the mark. Regardless, it was still an important semester.

I had met some interesting people. The thing was, I still hadn't made a major friend after the first few weeks. Then on Monday, I walked sixteen miles to buy a disc for disc golf, but when I got to the store, they were closed. It was the Monday of September 9th at one when I heard a strange loud knock on my door. It was Alan Baur.

He immediately asked, "Do you want to go get a wolf?" I had just started writing my first major paper and wanted to spend the day working so that I could go to my first SNU volleyball game as an SNU student. I put the homework away to go get a wolf. As it turned out, it was a coyote, but still cool. Alan drove us about ten miles to this coyote that was roadkill. I grabbed my gloves, and we put it in the truck. We then went back to campus, then we ran up and down the stairs of our dorm room asking guys what to do with this wolf. Alan and I ended up putting the wolf outside the window of some random girl's dorm.

It might seem insignificant, but that is how I met the man that would become my future roommate. Being flexible and willing is very important in college and is a great way to meet people. I missed the volleyball game that night. I did however look at the box score; SNU lost in three sets. Maybe I was glad I didn't go to the game. I talked to Alan, and we decided that we would find a local church and go as much as we could. We started going to May Avenue Church of the Nazarene. On September 22, 2013, I was part of a meeting with the pastor of May Avenue Church of the Nazarene, his oldest daughter, Alan Baur, Alan Miller who was a junior, and two other people.

The meeting was about starting an afterschool program at the church and doing Wednesday night kid night with local inner-city OKC kids. The daughter was going to be the director. Alan Miller and the other two would team up as the first interns at the church to run the after-school program. Baur and I would volunteer to watch the kids on Wednesday nights. It was hard to do, but I agreed. Luckily, I owned three footballs, two basketballs, a volleyball, and Baur had a soccer ball.

We became Wednesday night coaches. We had so much fun with those kids in the parking lot of that church. The interesting thing was most of the kids that showed up to play had never been on an official team and didn't know the rules of some of the sports.

By October 13th, it was time to see an SNU sporting event in person: I went to my first SNU football game. I sat at the top of the bleachers behind where the so-called student section was. There were seven students at the game, and they all seemed to have left by the end of the first quarter. In their defense, SNU was behind 31–0. I wanted someone to change just about everything about SNU athletics, but I did not think anything would change. Whoever started the change would be a hero. Little did I know what was to come. Something I had been studying in composition one was Joseph Campbell's Seventeen Stages of the Hero's Journey, and the second stage is the refusal of the call. I found myself in this stage.

CHAPTER FIVE: FIFA, FUN, AND FINALS

"Fear in a man's heart weighs him down, but a good word makes him glad."- Proverbs 12:25.

Fear, procrastination, and worry are three words that often cross the mind of a college student. This was very much true for me as my first semester went on.

It was October 20th at 10:00 p.m. At that time little did I know Alan Baur had signed me up for a hall FIFA tournament. I would soon become the luckiest FIFA player ever. I had spent all day working and had finished everything due for the week, when Baur unlocked my door and walked right into my room to tell me about this tournament. Now, this was odd for two reasons: First, I lived in 512, and he lived in 515; second, I didn't remember signing up for a FIFA tournament. First, to clear things up, every key in Snowbarger has a sister key somewhere in the building, so one key unlocks two rooms. It just so happened that Baur and I were put in rooms that were sisters.

It was like a sign from God that we should be friends. As it turns out there were eight people in this tournament, and seven people showed up. Let's just say I got past the first round by default. My next match was with Shawn. He was from my family group and was Alan Baur's roommate. I beat him three to nil. I continued playing, winning, and loving this. I got to the final. I was playing Ian. All of his games had been 7–0 skunks. It took me two overtime wins to get here. Most of the room was rooting for me in what would be a best of three. I gave up a goal in the first four minutes of game one, but that was the last goal I gave up all game. I scored in the ninetieth minute of the game. I ended up winning the first game in a penalty shootout. The second game I scored first but gave up a late goal. It looked just like the first game in reverse because this one also went to a penalty shootout. I won once again in a shootout. I was crowned the champion, and then we chose to play a third game just for fun. He beat me 3–0, showing just how lucky I had been all tournament.

It was moments like this that made me want to go to more SNU sporting events. I just couldn't bring myself to go because I was so afraid SNU would lose or would not want the support, or even worse, I would become a loser. If you think you want to do something, do it in college, and if you can sense something, go with it, because college is short. The fear of becoming a loser crossed my mind from time to time. Being out going open and trusting your gut is the best way to keep from being a loser. Also, it is important to try to have fun and work hard no matter what.

It was October 25th, the night of a dance. Some friends and I had decided to not go to the event. There is always a choice of what to do and were to go. It is important to go to class, and most school events are fun, but creativity is a big skill in college, as it can lead to fun. Alan and I talked for a short time. Soon, we decided to explore the Snowbarger vent system. We crawled around up there so much we got onto the roof. I tore my sweatpants having so much fun. I was also thinking of one of the strangest things when I was in the rafters. I thought about how many sporting events that I had missed, and that I wished I would pull myself up by my bootstraps and go to some games.

The next weekend I went to Nebraska. I went to an order of the arrow meeting with an Eagle Scout friend of mine from college. He asked me on Thursday, and I had to choose immediately. He was one of the people on campus at this time that had my full respect. He was an Eagle Scout who always seemed to keep his word and liked sports. He and I have a weird story of how we met. I was doing Wednesday nights coaching at the church, and he wanted to be part of an internship, so he came to visit the church to see if he wanted to be part of our inner-city work. When I was introduced to him by Alan Miller, he said to me, "He's the other one, Josh." I immediately hugged him; I almost squeezed all the air out of him as he was trying to figure out, "Other what?" We were the only two Eagle Scouts on campus. We had a great trip. College is made up of these great trips; don't start planning them now, but just know that when you have an opportunity to take a trip, do it. Also, short-notice college trips are great bonding and lifelong experiences.

Not long after that trip, it was time for the first basketball game of the season. SNU had always put homecoming with the first basketball game of the year because there might be a chance of SNU winning the basketball game. I went to the game. Before I get into what happened, I have to refer back to my Comp One class and learning about the hero's journey. The third and fourth steps happen together. The third step is finding a supernatural aid, or, as I like to think of it as, special gift from God. The fourth step is crossing the threshold. Both of these would happen to me the night I went to that homecoming game.

I was one of the first students to arrive. When I got there, I was handed a megaphone and asked if I wanted to help lead chants. With minimal hesitation, I said, "Absolutely." SNU started behind; they fell behind 9–0, and at the first timeout, students started leaving. After the timeout, SNU went down and got a dunk; it was 9–2, and I started the famous De-Fence chant as SNU came back on D. I felt it was crucial to get a stop. We forced a shot clock violation. Then we got a three-pointer, and the score was 9–5, but we fouled underneath the basket. It was a shooting foul. I had seen many college basketball games. I knew the importance of the student section when the away team was shooting free throws. I started chanting that the ball is very big, the rim is very small. I felt I made the shooter miss the first free throw. Then I started chanting again. Then they missed the second free throw. After missing the second free throw, we started to take control of the game. I started to find myself, I started to find the person who I would be and come to be in college. I saw a small window into the kind of super-fan I could be. We won the game 101–77. It felt great. I felt so alive.

When I got back to the dorm from the game, Baur was there, and he said that he wanted to show me a video. There were lots of quotes from that video that would become meaningful to me, but that night, when I heard make sure the work you do is great, it seemed to hit me. Also, in the upcoming weeks, I was asked about that game a lot as well as if I was going to go to the game on Thursday.

As it turned out, I had my last final on Thursday and didn't want to stay for some odd reason. I wish that I had because any more time in college would have been great. Ultimately, it had been a hard semester, but I had enjoyed myself from time to time. I had a lot to think about over winter break. Perhaps I had found who I was. The truth is, I knew it all along, and most people do. We all have at least three best friends. The first is God. God always knows what best for us even when we do not, and God always wants what it best for us. God also knows all about us, including each hair on our heads. Our next best friend is us; we have wants and needs, and each person will always know what their wants and needs happen to be. Somehow, we do not always know what is best for us like God shows. Also, we have people who are best friends and enjoy and help in life, but they only know our wants if we share these things with them. The best way to have great friends is to let God be a best friend; always think "What is really best for me?" and "How can I help and maintain relationships with others?" That can be big things, like going to Nebraska, or little things, like sitting together; ultimately, finding yourself is important.

CHAPTER SIX: WINTER JAM

"But pray that it may not happen in the winter." -Mark 13:18

This was the verse that was quoted at the beginning of the concert known as Winter Jam. Winter Jam was a concert where lots of Christian bands got together to put on a show. It was something the pastor of the church I volunteered thought it would be a good idea to take the inner-city kids to. They loved it.

I would start volunteering more with the church. It was Monday, January 6th, 2014. I was back at college, and I promised Allan Baur I would meet with him at 5:30 to eat dinner. We were the only two people in the cafeteria until the pastor we had been working with came in. He sat with us, telling us he hoped to find us up here. He wanted to tell us that the after-school program was in jeopardy. Two of the interns were quitting, and the after-school program had dubbed us as needed volunteers. He would need both of us to volunteer Monday, Wednesday, Friday, and we had to recruit other people to volunteer other days, because we had to have two volunteers a day, so we needed two people for Tuesday and Thursday. He also scheduled us to go to Winter Jam on February 1st. For about a week, every conversation Allan and I had involved the statement "Hey, would you be interested in volunteering?" Ultimately, we recruited three girls, and occasionally, Baur recruited some random girl to help. These girls would help just one time and always seemed to have a crush on Baur.

We were growing together as friends. We started going to an SNU sporting event every other week, leading the after-school program when the pastor wasn't there, and getting really good at disc golf. One of the most interesting things that I learned that semester happened on January 18th. I learned of a friend taking some time off college, in fact this person left on January 20th. People in college and in life are going to change and make their own decisions. You just have to make yours as well. If someone that is becoming or having the potential to be a close friend takes time off, or if a guy slaps you in the face just because he is having a bad day, all you can do is try to do what is right and best for you. If someone punches you in the face, they need to understand that they hurt you, but how you react is all up to you; asking them why or ignoring the situation could be best because if you get so upset that you pull out a gun and shoot them, then you are liable for that.

Soon, it was Sunday, January 20th. I remember that day very clearly. I helped load the car. I had on my church clothes all day, even after my friend's dad made a point to tell me to take them off before helping load. After my friend left, I walked three laps around campus, prayed, and played around of disc golf. I decided to make a bet with myself: if the Seahawks won the Superbowl then I would go to visit this friend over spring break, but until then, I had to buckle down studying, be a part of the after-school program, and help SNU sports any way that I could. When I heard Mark 13:18, I told myself I was not going to let this winter be a bad one; at least not for me, and my life. Do not let the winter be bad. Do what is best for you in your life. I endured that loud concert. I felt like I needed to cut out time to go to more SNU sporting events after the concert. This thought seemed to weigh on me as I got on the church bus and road home. I thought about SNU athletics the rest of the night until Baur told me about his predicament.

CHAPTER SEVEN: RUINED LIVES, MAYBE

"Therefore I tell you, whatever you ask for in prayer, believe that you have received it, and it will be yours." - Mark 11:24.

It was February 2nd at 6:00 a.m., when there was a knock on the door, and I knew it had to be Alan Baur. We went to the hall to talk; he didn't have anything to say but something to show me. As it turned out, he had adopted a child at Winter Jam. As for Baur, what we were praying for was something that he had received. It was an adopted child. I had hopes that it would go away or be safe without us somehow. I cried out at that moment. God, just help us take care of this life. As it happened, my roommate had gone home for the weekend, and so, Alan and I started to talk about what we have ended up financially responsible for. Alan would not be the only one to have troubles that day.

Alan and I spent the day trying to think of ways to make money for the kid he had adopted. The truth was, I had nerves about the Super Bowl to be played that night, and as it turned out, the Seahawks had made it…so, my bet was on. Soon, it was 5:00 p.m. and time to go eat. Baur and I were walking to the cafeteria, when he got a text from the pastor that he wanted to have dinner with us. We went to his place to eat. I told him about Baur and his dealing with the adopted kid.

After a short dinner, it was time for the game. Alan Baur and Alan Miller came over to my room for the game. Miller brought some sodas. Baur brought some chips. It was not that great of a game. The Seahawks won 43–8. I started planning my trip to visit that friend. Something to note: friends are important; it's not always what you do together but how you do it; it's also not always the who that matters but the why. Right as I was having some problems, some friends helped me. Friends are very important things in life because they can help with everything.

I was not the only person on campus having troubles. Another guy had been dating some girl he met in downtown. He claimed to be in love with her. They had been on two dates, and he was already talking about proposing. He was so involved in proposing that he wanted to drop out. *Did he want to DROP OUT of SNU?* my mind thought. He wanted to get a job at some plant to set up a payment plan for the ring. It was a ten-thousand-dollar ring. I started to think that he was going crazy. The other thing to know about the girl he was dating is she already had a ring from her ex-boyfriend that looked expensive. Baur pointed it out to me when she came to campus to visit, and he pointed it out again when we stalked her on Facebook. Sometimes, with friends, all it takes is a good talk; other times you have to help in odd ways. It was at a basketball game; I got an idea. I do not remember much about this game, but we seemed to help the team win the game because our obnoxiousness distracted the opponent. So, this was my plan to help our friend come back to reality. We would get obnoxious gifts and give them to our friend from his girlfriend and he would break up with her. This plan got shot down for many reasons. First, because Baur and I did not want to put any money into breaking them up. Second, she already was that way, always sending him stuff. We thought he might be lost.

Then it was February 14th, Valentine's Day. I had some anonymous girl send me cookies and flowers. When I took them to Alan's room to ask him to help me find out who it could be, we found a solution that would show how much our friend was "in love." We had a new plan. We put it into action. We took the cookies and flowers, got a girl to write a nice note to the guy telling him to bring his guitar and meet her in the gazebo, and we placed this on his desk. It kind of worked. As soon as the guy saw this, he grabbed the guitar and ran to the gazebo. We never told him that we set him up, but we did tell him if he was so worried about knowing who this girl was, then maybe he should break up with his girlfriend. He told us that he just wanted to know who she was. The truth was that he always seemed to hit on every girl that had feet. He also told us how he had proposed three times before and knew he just wanted to get married. He had lost all logic. He did not break up with his girlfriend, but he did the opposite: he dropped out the very next day. People will make their own decisions; we can just make our own decisions, like who we spend time with and how we spend our time.

As we were going through February, there were lots of basketball games. Alan and I made a pact not to miss a home basketball game. We ended up having a big impact on games. We really had something going for us, and the teams responded well to having some students in the stands. In fact, Alan and I got to witness SNU's first three-game winning streak in five seasons of men's basketball. That was not all the good news for that month as three kids in our after-school program had found Christ; life seemed great. At least until March 12th. I got some bad news that a friend of mine was in the hospital. It seemed important to have a good time with family over spring break. In college, getting time with family can be important, so knowing God can use all things for good is a factor in what to do next. My focus increased both on my studies and on making a March Madness bracket. I finished ninety-eighth in the ESPN bracket challenge. This helped my confidence some, but what helped the most was God's love. I had to pray. Then on March

23, after praying, I played one of my favorite speeches, and a quote hit me. "It takes courage to start over again. It takes courage to act." As I played this for Alan, we started talking about legacies as well as God's plan. We discussed the importance of getting new interns for our church, so we could focus on our Wednesday night deal once more. We could just be coaches and just have Wednesday to deal with. I could put more time into studying and other things; also, we needed help that would be more consistent. We might also go to more SNU sporting events if we had more interns to help us at our church. First, we were going to be even bigger fans next year; also, we would live in room 512 of Snowbarger next year. We both knew that the hall would have freshmen all over it, and we could mentor them as we tried to help the jocks. This last semester we had tried to help the jocks that lived on the fifth floor this year.

It was not long until we just had finals left. There was an end of the year party for our after-school program, and at this party was some girl I had never met before. The party was kind of lame, but there were some people, so I stayed. As the party was ending, some girl asked me if I wanted to go somewhere after this. I said yes! Going to hang out and making time for others is important; also, keeping a journal or something to keep these memories in is very important because just about anything can happen. All in all, the night was unique. We never saw those people again, but they gave us something to think about that summer. I took my last final the next morning. At that point, the semester was over, and the truth was, there was more to do in the ministry; we just had to follow God's path. We had lots of changes to make in order to improve SNU athletics.

CHAPTER EIGHT: MAGICAL

"Do to others as you would have them do to you."-Luke 6:31.

This Bible verse would come to represent how the friend group Baur and I came to be a part of. When Baur and I came back to school for our next year, we expected to be losers, but it was not that way. Many of the people I met in 2014 are people that I would run through a wall for; they are great people.

The story of these friendships started at the back-to-school bash. The bash took place on August 18th, 2014. Baur and I had spent the day moving into 512. It took all day because, as sophomores, there was no help from the yellow movers. Then it was time to go to the school bash, where we would meet some SNU football players. Baur and I were some of the best nine square players on campus that night. We were also the best cornhole players on campus that night. A good or lucky night can happen anytime in college; the best thing to do is to stay humble, because there was a lot of nights when I was not that great at nine square. We had loads of fun, and there are nights when fun needs to be the objective. It's also good to clear your mind before starting a new semester. We thought we might recruit some of the people we met that night to work with our church's after-school program. We also wanted people to go to sporting events with us. We wanted change, not only of the perception of SNUs sports but to help the athletes on campus as well.

As that week went on, I met Jace Bagwell, Brayden Burns, Christian Leeseberg, Quinten Foster, Greg Sattler, Jonathan Perez, Tanner Willson, Chase Grantz, Tyler Stark, Kyler Ross, Geoff Miller, and lots of other freshmen. The ones that lived together in Snowbarger were the "men of Snow" as we called it. We became much closer than the ones that lived in the dorm last year. The odd thing was, I met many of these men when I was naked. Let me just tell the stories. The day before the first day of classes, we had all finished enrolling when an upperclassman, an upperclassman who had become a spiritual leader on campus said, "Let's go for a dip in the Canadian River." He joked with me. Betting with me by saying I wouldn't take my bathing suit off and get naked, he lost. As we went up the river, he grabbed my bathing suit, hiding it from me. When we got back to the place, I started getting nervous. All those dreams of showing up at school naked seemed to be coming true, but he showed me it was all just a prank. Then, a few days later, another one was also a prank when I was in the shower, when Jase took my room key and went to my dorm room and locked me out, naked. I was out of the room for about an hour. I started doing calisthenics soon. Tyler got me a towel, and eventually, I got back into my room. You're going to meet new people; do not be afraid or ashamed of who you are, and never be afraid of making friends. Just being the best version of yourself is the best way to make friends. Those moments were the start of something I truly cannot describe using English words, but in Greek, the word is *philia*. Soon, it was September 4th, a day when I became enlightened. Let's just say I now know the three biggest things in life to balance are God, family/friends, and business. For me this meant balancing the church after-school program and Wednesday night activities, my family/the men of Snowberger, studies/helping SNU sports the best I could. In college, there is a lot to balance. Having a calendar or planner can make all the difference; budgeting time is really important because there is so much going on at one time. Even if it feels like a slow start to a semester; just know trials will start in some form or fashion.

"Surely the righteous will never be shaken; they will be remembered forever. They will have no fear of bad news; their hearts are steadfast, trusting in the Lord. Their hearts are secure; they will have no fear; in the end they will look in triumph on their foes. They have freely scattered their gifts to the poor, their righteousness endures forever; their horn will be lifted high in honor." -Psalm 112:6-9.

It was Saturday, September 6th, 2014, at 10:00 a.m. Baur and I were going to the cafeteria to eat breakfast. When we got there, the pastor of our church had a table ready for us and wanted to meet with us. He had called the potential interns and volunteers for the after-school program. Note, having some snacks in the dorm room can be super important because the cafeteria is not open twenty-four seven. Also note that not everyone you meet is going to be easy to work with. Being a helper can be important, no matter what, because it is that help that always seems to come back. When we do not help, it can come back in a bad way as well. There was this freshman that said that he would work as an intern if he didn't become the class president. The election was that day. He was a lot different form Allan and I, but we thought that the best thing to do was to try and help him win the election.

This day was becoming more important as it went on. The meeting ended at 10:45. I raced back to my dorm room to see the end of college gameday and to watch OU beat the crap out of Tulsa 52–7. It was not long after the OU game there came a knock on my door; it was that freshman, who said, "I'm officially withdrawing my name for the internship." He also asked if he could watch an Ohio State football game with me. They were playing Virginia Tech, who beat them 35–21. He was crushed. I told him we would help him if he ever needed us, but it was time for me and Baur to go to the SNU football game. The game was against Henderson State. I stood the entire game. Baur and I got the rosters of Henderson State and yelled at the players by name. Despite our enthusiasm, the game did not go our way; it was not easy, because SNU lost 72–7. The biggest part of support is maintaining positivity and to keep showing up.

Something about that freshman who ran for president, a story that's hard to tell is the blanket story. What happened is that some guys, I don't know who, but some took all the blankets from his bed. This is when I took action. I lent him a dorm sheet set. It included a bed sheet and two blankets. I knew he was never going to return them, but it was also the right thing to do. Soon, what happened to me after asking him about the situation, and he let people know what I had done. Not long after this, a mother made two blankets, one for me and another to give away to pass on God's love.

Then after the game, we had to keep our commitment to helping with the election. He had found out he lost the election and had started some kind of prank war with some goons. They had dumped water all over him. He led Baur and me into water, mud, and a gross fight. Trying to keep safe was not easy. Soon, Christian Leeseberg joined us. There can be some rowdy nights in college; if it's Nerf guns or water guns or something else, people can get into a big fight just trying to mess with one another. Keeping an open mind and keeping cool are important because you never know what's going to be thrown your way. Sometimes if you drop the ball trying to help in one way, helping another might be a good thing. We hadn't really help much with the election, in fact he had lost. Somehow picking his side in this water guns/prank war was important. Life will go on, but if you have the time allotted and something's going on, sometimes jumping in is simply the best thing to do, and that is just what we had done by joining the water fight. I was becoming more passionate about this topic, so much so that I was going to go to as many sporting events as I could. On Monday the 8th, I went to a golf event.

That Thursday the 11th, the men's soccer team had a game against Dallas Baptist. Baur and I went to the game and made a deal that every event we went to we would get the other team's roster so we could yell at other team players. I remember five minutes into the game two older women sat right behind me. As Baur and I were yelling things like "Pass me the ball, Mikie," or "Cut your hair, Jimmy," the girls started a conversation of their own. Remember when our mascot was the Redskins and there was the club the Redmen? They described the club as a bunch of rowdy boys that acted like Baur and I. The club got shut down because it didn't fit with the spirit of the school. Also, our name changed from the Redskins to the Storm. The women left after only ten minutes. After the 3–4 loss, Baur and I clapped for the team, trying to show support for their efforts. On the way back to the dorm, we talked about what those women had said. We asked questions like: "Should we quit? How do we do more?" We decided not to quit. We were going to do our best to support SNU athletics and try to help them win or encourage them when losing.

On Monday the 15th there was another men's soccer game. This time they were playing Colorado Springs. This is the game I remember as the RA game. A female RA and some of her friends sat two rows behind me. As they were walking up, Baur pointed out her. Then Baur told me stating she might not like us or what we do at these games. "We need to be safe tonight," he emphasized. I saw her talking with one of those ladies that sat behind us last game. As that game went on, I muscled myself more and more because every time I said anything, I looked back at her, and I couldn't tell if she wanted Baur and I kicked off campus, if she didn't care, or if she might have even seen us as funny. Nonetheless, SNU lost 4–0. The game was bad. Baur and I started to think that there might be people out there that did not like us. This was worse than becoming losers, because getting on probation would not be good.

There was a volleyball game against Midwestern State the next night. I remember cheering loud, and I truly felt I got into the other team's head, and with the game on the line, a bad serve led SNU to win the game three sets to two. It was nice to see SNU finally win at something. It was the next morning in my Composition Two class, when we started talking about trials in stories, it got me thinking about how Baur and I might be having some trials of our own.

Another one came as we searched for balance in our lives. I realized this the night of October 25th, 2014, at around 9:00 p.m. It was less than a week before SNUs annual Sadie Hawkins event TWIRP. Baur and I would not get asked, and I realized it that night. In a single moment, a group of guys knocked on my dorm room and said we had to run away; some girls were after us. I thought, *What are we, five?* Girls chasing boys to give them cooties? I said, "It's a boy's dorm. I think you're safe here."

They said, "No, we need to get caught, so we have to run somewhere else." We went to Christian Leeseberg's truck, but before we could get out of the parking lot, we looked at the girls running at us, holding some sign that had something written on it about ice cream. The purpose of the sign was for Becca to ask Christian Leesebergs to the TWIRP event. Her friends all seemed super interesting, but I did not have the time to talk with them. To tell you the truth, I really don't know why. Burns and I got asked to help some other girls ask some guys.

My favorite one was helping some girl ask Tanner Willson. She could not walk into our dorm due to restrictions and rules of the separation of male and female dorms. To say the least, SNU is super strict about boys and girls being in each other's dorms; they have very select hours. So, Anna had to stay down in the lobby. Burns and I just had to find a way to get Tanner to go down to the lobby so she could ask him. I had the idea to tell him that we were going on a donut run. He walked down the stairs in his Batman pajamas.

I started going to games; there were a lot of losses, but every win seemed memorable. Being supportive no matter what, I started to find real balance. Halloween has always been a holiday I enjoyed, but I enjoyed this one very much. Overall, that semester had been one big trial; it was good but not great. We still had to find a way to get more wins and get other people to games. SNU did not win a football game that season. The closest they came was the end-of-the-year homecoming game against Southwest Baptist. I gave it my best, but it was not good enough, as SNU lost 14–20. As I went to take my last final for that semester, my thought was not about the bigfoot presentation I was going to give but about what could I do to help SNU actually win more consistently. After that final, I saw a football player. He told me a quote I'll never forget. He said, "The team and athletes love you guys, and it makes us more welcomed on campus." However, I was not better, because there was still so much to do. I had an idea to make a club like OU had that was all about supporting the school athletics. I also wanted to google ways that fans impact every sport, so that Alan and I could be as useful as possible. I did lots of research over winter break and was ready for the next semester.

CHAPTER TEN: PARTICIPATING

"He gives strength to the weary and increases the power of the weak. Even youths grow tired and weary, and young men stumble and fall; but those who hope in the LORD will renew their strength. They will soar on wings like eagles; they will run and not grow weary, they will walk and not be faint."- Isaiah 40:29–31. I

It was January 3rd, 2015. Both SNU basketball teams had a game. I was the only student at both games. After watching the girls lose 49–55 and the boys lose 75–78, I felt bad. The next day, Baur came back to campus. I told him about the games. Then we strategized and talked about how to help the teams; we also played nine rounds of disc golf with an average of -4. We looked at some stats from the men's game, finding out that ECU went 61 percent from the free-throw line. If they had just missed three more, they would have shot less than 50 percent. If that happened, SNU could have won the men's game. I then did more research. Baur and I found out about Feinberg's theory of distraction. We YouTubed best free-throw distractions. We wanted to become the best free-throw distraction ever.

Soon, it was January 6th, and other students were moving back on to campus. That night we ended up playing games in Hills. Chase Grantz came into our room. He wanted to give input on our free-throw ideas. He told us that girls would never like me or Baur, because of who we were on campus. I asked what he meant. He said, "Girls likely just see you two as the odd sports guys." Those words hit me hard.

Baur responded, "We go to the games not to pick up girls, and that's not going to change no matter what."

As the days passed, Baur and I started getting back into the flow of things. The men won their basketball game 70–62, with help from us and our new spinny contraption. The spinny contraption was something that me and Baur made together. It was made out of a plate and paint. It looked like a hypnotist's evil spinning wheel, but it worked. When we showed up to church that Sunday, the pastor took the chance to talk to us. He wanted to say that the after-school program would be starting back now that we were back in town. The church gave us a standing ovation. As it turned out, over winter break there had been two shootings within a square block of the church. So, everyone at the church had been on edge. There would not be another shooting until after I graduated. Somehow, when we were there having the after-school program or our Wednesday night deal, the gangs in the area gave the church a wide berth.

On January 24th life started moving a little bit faster. We went to a skating event. Not being a strong skater, I spent most of the night on my butt and face. In college, it is not always how you do things but that you participate. My advice from this moment is from the movie the *Sorcerer's Apprentice*, when Jay Baruche's character is called out by his best friend for not getting involved enough. David Stutler Jay's character is told that he needs to participate. Even as I fell down, I ended up meeting people and hanging out with old friends, ultimately having a good time.

That's what I would do when the other team was at the free-throw line. Much like the curtain of distraction at Arizona State, I would have a good time, participate, and be myself.

Then on January 27th, Baur and I were playing disc golf. We were tied at -3 and starting the fourth hole, when a car stopped and two people got out and asked us if we wanted to take a ride with them. First, we had birdied the first three holes, and we were set up for a score way above our average. The fact that I even thought about leaving the game for what would happen next still baffles me. Baur said, "Yes, I'm ready to end this game anyway." We were then taken to Lake Overholser, where we went on to have a great interaction. I used to watch that event over and over in my memory. Participating means being flexible. If you are hanging around and people want to go someplace if you have the time, then going can be very important. These people made sure Baur and I had decided to go to the spiritual life retreat. This retreat started on February 6th. Thoughts got more traction at the men's basketball game on February 5th. It was a great game that night. I felt like I had a real reason to perform. SNU fell behind 82–84 with three minutes to go. I started a loud D-fence chant that led to a stop and a win. SNU won 94–84.

Friday was a very casual day. Baur and I had to be at the bus stop by 5:30 if we were going to go on the trip. I went to class, then spent the rest of the day doing homework; then as I was finishing an assignment for my US history class, I looked down at my watch. It was 5:17. I had packed my bag last night after the basketball game, so I grabbed it, and as I opened the door to get to the bus stop, Baur walked in asking if I had eaten yet. I told him, "No but we do not have time." So, we went to the cafeteria with paper lunch sacks that Baur got from Walmart for a rainy day. We made about seven or eight PB and Js, put them in the bag, and headed for the bus; our adventure had started.

It ended up being a long bus ride. When we got there, I realized I packed about nine flashlights. I did not want to deal with all these flashlights and started giving them away to some of my friends from Snowbarger. After giving out my flashlights, we sat through a moving sermon; it was about being the best you that you could be. I remember at the end of the sermon, I felt very warm and knew that the Holy Spirit had landed on me, and it would stay with me all weekend.

Then we were given two options. One option was to go outside and play some capture the flag; the other option was to stay inside as they were going to set up some board games. I couldn't turn down a game of capture the flag. We played three games. My team won all of the three games. We had just gotten lucky I suppose. I really enjoyed myself once again it was important to be participating. After the game, we were on our own for the rest of the night; the leader said to be up for breakfast at eight. A guy suggested that we toss around a volleyball on the front porch of the cabin that we were spending the night in.

We ended up tossing and volleying around for two hours. I was going all out, including diving for the ball. I might have been over participating at that point. After all, we were just hitting the ball around. At midnight, people started singing "Happy Birthday." At that time, it seemed odd, but soon, I would know why. After this, we decided to go inside and play with them. We played a round of the card game spoons before it was time to go to bed. As I was brushing my teeth, someone was reading an excerpt from the book Gideon. It hit home, as I discussed it with a major leader on campus. I told him how much of a spiritual leader he was on campus, and he told me someday I would be a major part of the campus. He said that thing that happened to you during the sermon is something that you can use at any time that you need to derive energy from God.

It was two a.m., and we had to be up at eight; I have kind of a superpower where if I tell myself I need to be up at a time. I can look at my watch and go to sleep, and I can wake myself up at that time exactly. So, I looked at my watch and said, "Let's go for seven-forty." I woke up at 6:41. Then I went outside to watch the sunrise. There were these three crosses, and I froze my butt off to watch that sunrise, but it was surreal as the sun came up behind the three crosses. I got ready for the day and sat in my bed until 7:55, remembering a quote from *Gettysburg* from Joshua Chamberlain:

"Hold to the last."

"To the last what?"

"Last shell...last man...last foot of ground... last breath." I felt that I had to hold the line that day. Growing up, for me, this meant ultimately following God's call no matter what, even when it would not be easy, and times were coming when it would not be easy.

As I got to breakfast, I realized I was the only one there. At eight some girls showed up, and they were there to serve breakfast. By 8:30 most people had shown up, and we were all eating together on long tables. We were talking about last night some. Baur and I were bragging about our disc golf scores and finishing up eating. Then someone came up to me and asked: "Would you like to finish this for me?"

As they looked me in the eyes, I said, "Absolutely." It was those small moments that make friends and come out of participation. I felt all warm again suddenly knowing I was ready for the day. As we left, we were told by the pastor of the place, "You have an hour to explore, then come back to pack up. There will be another talk, and I'll send you back to SNU restored."

I was in pants, and I asked the guys if they wanted to go for a swim. Then I took off my pants to reveal my bathing suit, but the boys wanted to play board games, then go somewhere to pray, or some other option that I didn't hear. Baur said that he wanted to hike and then maybe swim in the lake. We hiked up some hill and found some river with an abandoned canoe. I had my Bible with me and took a moment to pray as we were paddling around that pond. Truthfully, we had a great hike, and it got better as we lost track of time and had to run back. We were like squirrels going across trees. We went so fast. Then we had to skid down some rocks to get back to the cabin. It was so hard, and I hurt my arm so badly. I packed up super-fast, then went down to hear the final sermon. This one was about how people are angels, and it's important to follow God even when that leads us down a well-worn path. He also encouraged us to talk about what we thought life was about.

We got on the bus at the end of our long bus ride and great talk. A girl invited Baur and I to her birthday party that night. We got back to school that afternoon. We got back just in time for Baur and me to go to SNU's baseball game. It was a great game; we got into the game big time. It ended up going into extra innings, and in the tenth inning we were mocking the other team's number ten; this led him to strikeout. Then SNU had the momentum they needed to win. SNU beat William Jewell Mo. 10–9. That night I did not go to the basketball games. I went to her birthday to play Cranium. I was not my usual competitive self. Always try to be yourself. Participating is important, but you are not fully participating if you do not be yourself. If I had been myself more, I know I have had more fun. "Behind every principle is a promise"—Eric Thomas. I learned a very big principle that weekend. Participating is not a one-time thing but a full-time thing. It's not just being goofy one time or using your spiritual gifts when you feel comfortable. It's giving every moment to God and letting God make you into who God wants you to be. In fact, it was that weekend that I discovered something about myself. I discovered that I could write a poem off the top of my head like magic. We can be ourselves and use our spiritual gifts and try to come popular, yet, ultimately, God's in control, and we have to remember and respect that and try to be ourselves. That night I had not really been who I was hit me hard, but know that a reset is coming, and a chance to be yourself again.

SNU, it turned out, did not have a home game until Thursday, February 19th. Later the night of February 8th, because I couldn't sleep, I cleaned up the room, finding the book that a girl had given me back two Halloweens ago. I spent every available moment that I had reading that book as well as perfecting my ability to create a poem off the top of my head. So, once again I put myself into my studies, the church, and SNU athletics.

On the 19th, just before the women's basketball game, I looked in the crowd to see lots of people. The girls lost 73–74, but it should not have been that close. I did not do my best at distracting the other team. This would not happen again. I had to start being myself once more. I felt like I had a job to do, and no one could keep that from happening. The boys were also heavy underdogs, but they won 96–90. I learned I just had to let go and trust in God. I also wanted to do whatever it took to no longer be a loser and remain SNU's biggest fan. That was who I was. My strength was greatest when I was at games and that is how I was participating.

CHAPTER ELEVEN: HEROES OR VILLAINS

"But the word of the Lord endures forever. And this is the word that was preached to you."-1 Peter 1:25.

Life is all about perseverance. I learned this with what happened as my sophomore year fleshed out. I also learned what makes a real-life hero.

All of a sudden, it was March 6th, when Baur and I were playing some disc golf. Planning out the games we were going to go to, along with lesson planning for the after-school program and talking about life. Then, all of a sudden, I started getting engulfed by the golf game I was playing my best game ever, and I scored a -6. We went to the tennis game on the 11th that Wednesday. SNU beat Ouachita Baptist 6–3. We felt like we behaved well and had an impact, but soon, we got an email from a major administrator saying that we had a mandatory meeting with them. That fear of being more than losers and winding up on probation was actually coming somewhat true. Our meeting didn't go well. They told us that we could be put on probation or kicked off campus if we were misrepresenting SNU. They said that, personally, they thought we were doing a great job and loved seeing us at games. We didn't feel like heroes. Just after that meeting, Baur and I were checking our emails, and we had an email from Timothy Riggs. I thought, *Oh crap, what is going on? We need to start working on transferring.* As it turned out, he wanted us to help him relaunch the Weathermen, a club that would be a group of people that would be the biggest fans on campus and would help grow SNU's student fanbase. We accepted but never had a meeting to discuss what it meant. He was just married and "super busy." This was the club that I had thought about earlier. One thing he said in his email gave me something to work for: he called us heroes.

After March 30th, Baur and I cheered on the baseball team to a 4–3 upset of the number-one team in the country and a rival, Oklahoma Baptist. We then had another meeting with a different administrator. We were told they knew about the formation of the weathermen and our importance to the athletic program. This led to a discussion with Baur; we thought if we transferred to a non-Christian school we would be heroes.

ECU and UCO came up as places we could transfer to. We even printed off transfer paperwork. We realized that as pleasing as the idea of transferring to be liked, it was not the most honorable thing to do. I found myself once again in this paradox of wanting to be liked, but also SNU's number-one fan. I thought of Paul and how he suffered, and I just thought we belonged at SNU, but maybe taking some time away from sports was just what we needed. The temptation to take the easy way is always prevalent, but Baur and I knew we had to be heroes.

Soon it was Good Friday, April 3rd, when I went to church and had written part of the program. It just so happened that night a local gang member showed up and got converted. After witnessing this, I felt like we were doing God's work and were in the right place. There were many volleyball, disc golf, and basketball games that Baur and I played getting ready to watch sports. Summer was coming, and as summer shows up, college can get a little more intense as finals draw near. With the extra pressure, slowing down to focus on school is a good thing. Also finding ways to stay in touch over the summer is very important. A group of guys got together, and one day, every time we walked by Chase Grantz's door, we would a screw out of it, and at the end of the day we took the door off, so when he came back from his night class there was no door on his dorm room. Little pranks can lead to the exchange of phone numbers and a good laugh to clear the stress of finals. Life seemed great as the semester was coming to an end. Baur and I had decided to enroll in another semester even if we were seen as villains.

CHAPTER TWELVE: RUSES

"Therefore encourage one another and build each other up, just as in fact you are doing."- 1 Thessalonians 5:11.

I had made a friend at the end of that semester leading us to the events of April 8th, 2015. That was the day a new friend and I went to the casino. I walked in with twenty dollars, but I walked out with seven hundred dollars in cash. I had won big. I stuck the money in my desk. It seemed that the end of the semester was going to be a rollercoaster. Not long after I stashed the money in my desk, Baur showed up. He had gotten us a meeting with the athletic director, the new head football coach, and a recruiter. After our meeting, I learned that they all wanted to market the Weathermen as SNU's top fans. This was the deal they made with us. We could pick two people from each class who would sign up for a mission. A mission to attend as many sporting events as they could and represent SNU in an upstanding way. We had two Weatherman contracts, one that Baur signed and one that I signed. We were to turn these contracts in at the SGA room sometime that week, but at that moment, they were closed. I ended up playing volleyball for the rest of the night.

I played with some of the coolest people in the world, but when everyone is being themselves it's fun to hang out. I was surprised, to say the least. I also learned that someone was short lots of money on her bill for her summer Sims trip. Then what happens next ends up being, well, a call from God. It took me some time, but eventually, I donated the money that I won when I was at the casino to that Sims account. At the same time this was happening, Baur and I were trying to make a list of who we thought we should recruit to join the weathermen.

Later that week, Baur and I played some disc golf. He shot seven under and we decided to take it to Corban, the librarian, and he looked for scores on the disc golf course, and as it turns out, he could not find a list of scores that were better than under seven, so Baur claimed it as the school disc golf course record. When we got back to the dorm room, Brayden Burns, Kyler Ross, and Greg Sattler ran into our room telling us about a very important meeting that we needed to be a part of. The meeting was to arrange living arrangements for next year. I knew that things had to change. I simply was tired of going up all the stairs each and every day. The stairs were starting to take a toll. After passive-aggressive negotiations, it was decided that some of the guys would move to Hills, and the rest would take up residence on the third floor of Snowberger. When it came to draft day, we seemed to get exactly where we wanted most. Draft day was the day when people picked were to live next year on SNU's campus.

Soon it was the week of April 27th, 2015. That week I spent living life getting better at my poetry gift, getting destroyed in a FIFA tournament. Baur and I had been tornado/storm chasing (the real kind of storm chasing, not just going to sporting events). I had a meeting scheduled with one of the football coaches. The meeting was scheduled for the 27th. I had a summer job working maintenance for the athletic department at OU, and like me, many of my friends were going home for summer. When I got to the meeting, the coach asked me to sit down. Then asked me, "What does it mean to be SNU's biggest fan?"

I answered by asking, "Do you think that's me?"

He said, "Absolutely, so how is it?"

I then told him, "It's an honor." He told me that was great, then showed me a film that he had of me at various sports dancing, cheering, and distracting the other teams. He then told me that we needed more spirit like that. He knew about the Weathermen club, and knew it wasn't getting off the ground; he said to just invite people to the games and see what happens. It was the best advice ever. He also asked about my semester, wanting to know how my grades were, my summer plans, how life was, but the big thing was he wanted to know was if the athletic department could use this footage for recruitment. I told him he could; he also told me that he looked forward to seeing me in the stands that fall. It gave me a feeling of atonement.

On May 6th I took my last final at eight a.m. When I got out at nine a.m., I had my car already loaded, so I drove home. I had enrolled in a Vietnam history class at OU that summer; something that the professor of that class was obsessed with was rain and poor planning. It turned out that when studying about Vietnam, it rained almost every day that summer. I also had the first jury duty of my life that summer, after getting my jury duty assignment moved away from a school time. I visited Baur up in Kansas, spending time with him. I even went to Alabama to visit family, but it was a very boring summer; so boring that with twenty-one days left of summer, I started a countdown paper that I used to count down the days. However, there was something I learned in my Vietnam class that I would put to use, and that is how to plan.

As part of my job doing athletic maintenance, I was assigned to renumber each seat in the OU's volleyball arena McCasland Field House. I had lots of time to myself; lots of time to think and plan. I wanted five things for next semester. One, a couch for my dorm room; two, a chance to go to some OU football games and at the same time being SNU's number one fan; three, I wanted to keep up the after-school program at my college church; four, making good grades; five, spending quality time with my friends. So, a plan arose on how to accomplish this.

As I started thinking about this, a crazy scheme came to my mind. My father and I had talked earlier that week, and he told me what games I could get an extra ticket for. I then got to negotiating and ended up getting four tickets to the West Virginia game, and an extra ticket to the Iowa State game. I knew that there were lots of people at SNU that were OU football fans, so plans and counterplans started to come about in my head. I knew that Brit Dawson, one of the guys that I had started hanging out with, was a huge OU football fan. So, I got to thinking that I could give him two of the West Virginia tickets. I just had to find a way to convince Dawson I was getting a fair shake. One of the things I like about him is one of his strengths was fairness. I thought it was too bad I couldn't give him one ticket for his couch. If Dawson did not have a couch to trade, then I would be very convinced that he was getting a good deal, and I might take the extra Iowa State ticket for a couch from someone. Now I had a way to get a couch. I figured out how to go to some OU games and planned to go to lots of SNU games; I planned a schedule to study that allowed time to volunteer for the after-school program, knowing that I would have plenty of time to spend with friends. The biggest thing was getting on Dawson's schedule. I knew I had to ask early because he was a good scheduler, but if he was booked, he would stick to his schedule, so I knew to ask him early. It would all play out at the start of the next semester.

CHAPTER THIRTEEN: STREAKS

"But above all, my brothers, do not swear, either by heaven or by earth or by any other oath, but let your 'yes' be yes and your 'no' be no, so that you may not fall under condemnation."- James 5:12.

I picked this verse because it is about doing, and this chapter's going to be all about doing.

I moved into my dorm that year on the 25th of August, but things started getting interesting on 8-29-2015. That night was the back-to-school bash, and just before it, I went to Brit Dawson's room. After he said hi, I sat down on his couch. I told him about how much I liked the couch, and he said he was not going to keep it for very long because he was getting a new one. Could this get any better! I got super excited! I thought back to my plan. I traded two of the West Virginia tickets for that couch. They would get the third ticket, but that had to wait. First, I was not sure if I wanted them to get the third ticket, and also, it was time to bash. Yes, once again we headed to an SNU back to school bash.

Then, on August 30th, I was trying to figure out who I wanted to give that third ticket too. In order to think I played three rounds of disc golf with Baur. That third game we thought might be our best games ever played we both got -7s. A new course record. Baur and I also talked about new distraction techniques and ways to get new fans to games. We also once again had to replace two of May Avenues interns. We talked about potential prospects. These conversations would be put into action starting with Wednesday night September 2nd. I went to church that night to do my usual thing with the kids of the church. There were also three prospective interns. That night was started with a Bible study for the kids. I did a great job with that, then we took the kids outside and had them play games with these three. The pastor also talked to them and ended up offering them an internship. One took it right then.

We then would start recruiting another potential intern we liked. The next night was a sports night. It was the first women's soccer game and the first football game.

The soccer game was at four p.m., and the football game was at seven p.m. I managed to make both. The soccer game was close. We were playing Eastern New Mexico; they had this number ten. I hit on her/yelled/did anything I could do to make her mess up. She ended up missing three shots that night, and SNU won 1–0. Then it was time for the football game. It was not close. SNU lost 14–62. I remember the end of the game. In the movie *Bull Durham*, Crash Davis, played by Kevin Costner, talks about not messing with the winning streak. SNU football was having the opposite problem, as some of the other sports were doing well. Crash's quote goes for anything in life. If you think you're having success, don't mess with it. If it's because you're wearing strange underwear or breathing through your eyelids. Whatever you think, stick with it. I talked about participating, being yourself, sticking it out, loving others, but now I'll talk about riding the wave. Meaning putting it all together to get to a goal.

Then on the 7th of September, I was just sitting in the cafeteria eating dinner, when this girl just randomly sat by me. She then told me she was interested in working the after-school program at my church and wanted to know when she could help. I just told her to show up on Wednesday night on the 9th. I remember that night vividly. Sometimes riding the wave means going with life as well as trusting in God. We needed another intern, and it was as if one had just fallen out of the sky.

As it turned out, she was at almost every after-school event that the church had. This led us to Thursday, the 10th of September. That morning I was having breakfast with some friends when the pastor walked in to ask to talk to me on my way to class. He wanted to get my thoughts on bringing the worship band back to the church, and he wanted me to recruit one more consistent volunteer for the after-school program. I thought about that a lot that day. It hit me the hardest after that night's soccer game. A game that SNU won, beating West Texas A&M 2--0. This put the girls on a winning streak, making me feel great. There was a moment in the game that sticks out to me in my memory. It came like a role in the win as I got the crowd into the game, helping SNU get momentum at crucial times. After I was leaving, a person grabbed my shoulder. They had something to tell me, and it came out in a soft slightly gravelly voice as they said to me, "You're the guy. If there is anything I could do for you, I would." Then I just blurted out saying, "Well, I need help with a church after-school program." They ended up signing up after I gave them the pastor's number.

That night I got to my dorm room, and as I closed it, there was a knock. The guys wanted to know if I wanted to go to McDonald's to celebrate Brit Dawson's birthday. I thought that would be a great idea. As I was checking my email that night, I got an email from Samantha thanking me for my sports game enthusiasm. Samantha also wrote in the email the fact that there was a rise in attendance among students, and she had started advertising all over campus also helping. I seemed to be on a positive streak.

Then it was September 12th. At 6:00 p.m., I was watching two football games: SNU at Harding and OU at Tennessee. SNU lost 0–42. I felt so helpless in watching that game. SNU needed some kind of IT factor, something like Sooner magic. Yet in that moment, OU seemed to have run out of Sooner magic. Joshua Dobbs had just put Tennessee up 17–0. The dorm seemed to shake at that very moment with negative yelling as SNU was losing 30–0 at the half, and OU was behind. This was because given the fact that lots of people that lived on our floor were big OU fans. It seemed everyone was mad. Also, the people that were not OU fans wanted the halls to calm down. They even threatened to call the RD to give us all a noise fine. This was when our RA called us all into his room, so that if someone was going to get fined for being loud, it would be him. It was at that moment when the magic came back. OU got a field goal to end the quarter.

Then we watched and waited through a scoreless tired and a long fourth that was almost over. Then two TDs came for OU, one with 8:20 to go and the other with 0:40 left to go. OU tied the game and sent it to overtime. We got louder, but we were making positive noises now. After trading TDs in the first overtime, OU won in the second with a TD and then INT. I did a lap around the dorm after the win. It felt great to feel the magic; also, it was good to know that there were lots of sports fans on campus.

I sent an email idea of ways to advertise SNU sporting events around the campus as well as through the town. Life still happened; for instance, on Thursday the 17th, I met future President Trump as he was having a campaign rally at the Oklahoma State Fair. My roommate Baur even got to shake his hand. We were also taking the time to worship God as we made a point to not miss a Thursday night kingdom come. One of the things that I prayed about that night was that SNU would have better attendance. It happened SNU's attendance went up 10 percent over that semester and 35 percent of student attendance was up at basketball games.

It all seemed to start 9-19-15, when I volunteered my car to drive people to Ada Oklahoma and watch this away game in person. I had a full car. It was great. We did our best to cheer on the team, but they lost 69–0. This extended SNU's football losing streak to twenty-seven; the longest losing streak in NCAA history was thirty-four. We had to win one game this season or we would break that streak. To add insult to injury, a guy named Jordan shot a -7 on the disc golf course that night, so he joined Baur, and I tied with the record.

The next week SNU did not have a home game until Thursday, so I got some disc golf in, and it paid off. Because of what happened Tuesday the 22nd. I shot -8, becoming the sole owner of the disc golf course record. Talk to Corbin if you don't believe it. SNU lost both of their home games that week. Volleyball lost in three sets, and the football team lost 7–41. However, the women's soccer team continued their home winning streak as they beat our biggest rival Oklahoma Baptist 4–0. I did not think there could be a better game played, and I do not remember the stands having more people in them then that night. I did great, but the fact that we had major school leaders there helping me out showed how far SNU had come. I'll never forget what was said to me after that game. "The campus is starting to love you and how you're coming into your own." It led me to feel like I had no more problems being SNU's number-one fan.

On October 2nd, the men's soccer team was back in action, and it was the night before OU hosted West Virginia. That night was also a blood moon. I went to the soccer game, and it was not a good one. SNU lost 1–5, but when they scored, there was a crowd of people screaming for a goal, and as they left the field, there was a crowd of people to clap for them as they left the pitch. My friends and I were kind of upset about the game, and I needed something to take my mind off of tomorrow's event. Some people just wanted to look at the moon, but ultimately, we decided to play our own soccer game under the moon. I was placed at goalie because of how bad a soccer player I was; I remember a corner kick that I tried to defend where the ball went off my head and hit the post and went in for an own goal. At that moment, I heard someone say I could not curve a ball that way if I tried. I just responded, "That's why I'm in the stands and not out there playing." The next day I got up to think about the game and the people I was going with; let's just say it did not turn into that big of a story. OU won 44–24, and all my friends seemed to have fun, and life went on. I did feel bad about one thing: I missed the SNU football game that day, and they lost 20–55.

As that next week continued things were topsy turvy. The women's soccer team ended their home winning streak losing 0–2 on the 8th; volleyball had back-to-back victories on the 9th and 10th, but football lost a road game 10–51. The next week was more of the same. Women's soccer lost two out of their three home games. Men's soccer didn't win a game, but the golf teams both came in fourth place at their events. By that Thursday I was ready for fall break. Baur and I had discussed going back to his place for that fall break; it ended up being a great idea. That Saturday and Sunday would be good in the sporting world for me. OU beat Kansas State 55–0, and I got to see the Royals beat the Blue Jays 14–2, taking a 3–1 lead in the ALCS. It was the kind of rejuvenation that I needed. When we got back from fall break, Baur and I were ready to follow the women's soccer team on the road to Shawnee, Oklahoma, to face off against rival OBU. Baur and I got there, and during warmups, we asked any of the OBU players if they remembered us; we had thrown them off their game last time. That would not be the case as much this time. At halftime, the game was 0–0, so, in the second half, we started just randomly yelling goal when they had the ball; when we had the ball, it was time for our signature SNU chant. Eventually, we got a score, winning the game late with a final score 1–0.

That next week was Pink Out week and Homecoming. Men's soccer beat semi rival Oklahoma Christian 2–1; volleyball beat Harding in three sets; women's soccer beat ECU 1–0; but football ended the streak of wins for SNU athletics, losing 20–49. It was also a gold-out instead of a pink-out because pink was not cool enough for football or something like that. I hated that game because the team we were playing against had gold in their color scheme. We also needed a way to lead them, and the weathermen just had not come about yet. It was time to give that another good try. I talked to different people on campus about the weathermen. They just ignored it or told me maybe next year, but for now, they were swamped. That Halloween was also a riot.

The Royals took a 3–1 lead in the World Series, but SNU lost all kinds of road sporting events making me feel down so to cheer me up Baur took me to OKC. We just walked around looking at people's costumes, talking to people, and some other things happened that just helped me prepare for that Sunday. It was our church's fall festival. Baur was interested in the volunteers, the members of the church, and we had all worked hard on this putting in lots of stuff to make this great. We had even gotten a dunk tank together for the kids, and as it turned out, I volunteered for the dunk tank. Also, I will never be entering a dunk tank again. The important thing is the kids had fun. To tell you the truth, the after-school program had ended gang activity in the area. It had totally stopped, and in the month of October, two kids in the after—school program accepted God.

This got me thinking more about the book of James. His one-liners like, "Let your yes be yes, and let your no be no," as well as the message of James to have actions with your faith, and how important it is to speak well. I wanted to live this out as this was me as I was leaving the festival and started to pray. Then the pastor invited me to a prayer meeting every Sunday at eight a.m. I never missed one the rest of that semester.

That Monday, the 2nd of November, the JV basketball team beat Hillsdale Baptist 95–83. On Tuesday the volleyball team won in four sets; the women's basketball team beat Southwestern Christian 75–59, and the men's basketball beat McPherson 103–64. All those games went great, the fans were great. Baur and I started using the spinning things once again at the basketball games.

We were what you could call a sight. There was a girl in that game that went 0–5 from the free-throw line that night. Something Baur and I did was switched sides at halftime, so that the away team was putting their faces in front of our faces when shooting free throws.

That night there was a large celebration where we had our annual bond fire. There was lots of dancing and games that were played that night. I also hung out with the group to watch the movie *Wolverine*. SNU athletics was on another winning streak. Then it was time for the football game. SNU lost 7–58. That made the losing streak thirty-three; if they did not win the next game, they would tie the Northwestern Wildcats thirty-four-game losing streak. That next week, SNU Athletics won two in a row, starting with volleyball, beating Southwestern Oklahoma

State in three sets, and women's basketball beat St. Gregory's 77–70. That Thursday in class, a girl on the soccer team told me how cool it was that I did what I did and that I must be SNU's number-one fan. She asked me if I was called to do that; thinking back to James, then saying yes, my face lit up. She said, "Well, you do a great job, but it would be super great if SNU won their football game this Saturday, as it is the last one of the year." I had a very similar conversation with a basketball player that Friday. SNU had to beat rival OBU somehow and get a win on a senior night or I might just give up on being an SNU fan.

Then it was Saturday, November 14th. That morning I went to eat breakfast. I talked to Christian and Becca about the game. I distinctly remember her saying, "You said at the beginning of the year we were going to win this one we had to beat OBU." I also remember Christian telling me that if SNU won, he would help me start up the Weathermen's club and be a member. Soon, the game kicked off, and it got crazy fast.

SNU took the lead off of a John Martin fifteen-yard pass from James Mauro. Then with one minute thirteen left to go in the half, we got a safety, going up 9–0. SNU seemed to have control of the game; we scored on the next drive going up 16–0. In that half, I felt SNU should be up more. I ended up yelling at the referees and the other team. Our team was super loud; so loud that another fan had to grab me and tell me to slow down and win. That halftime I started having flashbacks to a high school playoff game where my school went into the locker room up 16–0 and lost in eight overtimes. After thinking about this I talked to Baur, we needed to go into the endzones when the opponent was in the red zone to try to distract them. It worked on the first drive, as OBU had a missed field goal one of two that quarter. We seemed to have their number, but for whatever reason, we couldn't finish a drive, and OBU was taking advantage of that getting TDS and two-pointers. At the end of the third quarter, OBU took the lead 20–16. It was time for SNU to step up.

We responded fast on a long pass, taking the lead 23–20. Soon there were thirty seconds to go when OBU took the lead, but Baur and I called out that kicker, and they missed the extra point, so it was 26–23 with thirty seconds to go. I went back to the stands, and during a time out I got an SNU chant going; it worked, and we sent the game to OT after a wild drive and a long Carlos field goal. We got a TD on our first drive, taking the lead 33–26. We won after OBU missed a two-point conversion, 33–32. We had broken the streak! We rushed the field. It felt a lot like Sooner magic as the streak was broken. I had ridden the wave sometimes; life just happens around you, and if you're doing your best, it's like riding a wave.

CHAPTER FOURTEEN: LUCK AND CHANGE

"The LORD turns his face toward you and gives you peace."- Numbers 6:26.

The week after the OBU upset game was great for me. Players walked up to me thanking me. Other students were telling me that Ttey were not going to miss a game next year. Some said that they wanted to be part of our project. Even coaches talked to us about how cool it was to have some good fans to be a part of that last game. I felt so peaceful, and the best part of that week was the meeting I found myself in.

Monday, November 16th, 2015. I had a meeting with one of the captains of the football team. He first wanted to tell me that I had an impact on them this season, making the players be more wanted on campus. He wanted to know what the players could do to be more a part of campus, and I told him about the athlete's chapel, and that they needed to participate in that. It would become a great chapel. I also had a meeting with Conor, another one of the captains of the football team. He wanted ideas of how the players could connect with the local town more. Without hesitating, I told him about the church I went to, and we ended up getting seventeen players to volunteer for the after-school program for the last few weeks of that semester.

Another meeting I ended up having that week was the Tuesday with Sam, the SGA lead athletic relations member. She wanted to talk about goals. She wanted to know what the idea of the weathermen would be, and she wanted to know how we felt about the theme night she had created for some sporting events for next semester. She also shared her ideas for next year if she was re-elected to her position. She wanted anyone and everyone to be a member. She also had a huge budget to use for unclear things. She did not seem very high on my idea to get a local meteorologist to announce the starters at a sporting event. She didn't like the fact that I wanted to change sides at the half of every basketball game. We did agree on the fact that it would be nice to have some money to spend on this club. Supporting SNU athletics would be that main goal, and we would go to as many sporting events as we could.

I ended up seeing her at the basketball games on November 21st, only four days later. Those games got good. She was into the game, but not even as close to being into the games as Baur or I was. The fans seemed few and far between. After I thought we turned the corner, it seemed sad, but SNU won both games against Ouachita Baptist. The girls won 75–62, and the boys won 87–74.

As I organized the club for Sam, it turned out that the rest of that semester she was super busy, and we never had a meeting again that semester, but it was atoning watching some of the late semester events at SNU, and going to Stillwater to watch OU beat Oklahoma State, but the day I took my last final was the day I had another problem. I went to the girls' basketball game against semi rival Oklahoma Christian. I was one of two students that were there. Another thing that happened that day is after the game, I went to eat dinner and was going to sleep one more night in my dorm bed before going home for winter break.

The pastor said he wanted me to run by his home for an emergency meeting. When I got there all the interns, Baur and the director of the after-school program were sitting around his dinner table.

I could tell that this would be an important meeting. As it turned out, the director was so far along in her pregnancy that she could no longer be the director of the after-school program. We were either going to have to recruit a new director/appoint a new director or temporally discontinue the program. Baur and I did not think we were qualified for this job, but we asked around talking to people that had volunteered with us before.

The thing that bugged me was none of the interns wanted that job. It had been a great week for the after-school program as one of the members of that community had committed her life to Christ. She had also started to turn her life around. She was a drug addict and one of the grandmothers of one of the kids that I worked within the after-school program. After his parents fell on hard times, he lived with his grandmother. Every day for a year, when he came home from the after-school program, he would talk about Jesus and what that lesson was or how nice the people of the church were. After she started visiting the church, she checked herself into recovery and started working with the pastor on stopping drugs, which she would do eventually.

As SNU did not have a home sporting event at all during that winter break, I spent it trying to find a way to keep the after-school program together. On December 31, I had a long phone call with the pastor and Baur. We had found a way to keep the kids of our after-school program going to an after-school church program. We paired with a group called Jubilee. They ran their own Jesus-based after-school program. The thing was, they only used their staff, and because Baur and I were not official staff members, we could not work for them.

The after-school program might have well been discontinued. Baur and I made our peace with that because we still got to do Wednesday night things with the church. Another thing that I did over break was made new spinny things for sporting events as well as exchanging emails with Baur about plans of things we would do that might get people to games and get them fired up to be there.

On January 5th, 2016, Baur and I got back to the dorm room at ten p.m. that night. The only thing that we did that night was recite the apostles' creed. Those words would echo in our minds as that semester went on. The words "I believe in God, the Father Almighty, creator of heaven and earth. I believe in Jesus Christ, God's only Son, our Lord, who was conceived by the Holy Spirit, born of the Virgin Mary, suffered under Pontius Pilate, was crucified, died, and was buried; he descended to hell. On the third day he rose again; he ascended into heaven, he is seated at the right hand of the Father, and he will come to judge the quick and the dead. I believe in the Holy Spirit, the holy catholic Church, the communion of saints, the forgiveness of sins, the resurrection of the body, and the life everlasting. Amen."

CHAPTER FIFTEEN: THANATOS

"If we live, we live for the Lord; and if we die, we die for the Lord. So, whether we live or die, we belong to the Lord." Romans 14:8

Soon it was January 7th, 2016, and the first day of classes of the spring semester of my junior year of college. It was also SNU's first home game in a long time. It was also a day with two basketball games. A women's game and then a men's game, both against Arkansas-Monticello, who was ranked in both, so I knew they would be some hard games. The girls' game was a doozy. It got off to a great start; SNU took an early 7–0 lead, and Monticello missed their first three free throws, but they fell short, losing 74–83.

Even though they lost, I still felt that it was an okay game as they went head to head with a ranked team for a big game. I decided that I would have to crank it up a notch for the men's game.

The boys won the game 80–64; they looked the best they ever had. They also had a large crowd show up, leading me to start thinking about the major divide between the crowd at the women's and men's games. I wanted to do something. I took it to the gender equality club, but nothing ever seemed to change. We advertised the same amount as for the men's game.

On the 12th of that month, I played my first disc golf game since shooting the -8. That night I shot +3, it was bad, but it was the next night that I got some information that affected my mind-set for the rest of the semester. It was that night that my father called me to tell me my grandpa, whom I called Pops, had a doctor's diagnosis saying that he had three days to three months to live. I was thinking about that all day on Thursday the 14th until it was time to go to the basketball games that night. Northwestern Oklahoma State was the opponent for both men and women. The women's game became legendary.

It was back and forth from the start. NWOS did not shoot their first free throw until forty-nine seconds left in the first quarter. They missed, but they rebounded and got fouled again, going to the line for two free throws making the first, but missing the next. This led SNU to have the lead at the end of the quarter 20–18. The next time they shot free throws was with fifty-six seconds left in the half, and they made both. After the girl made them, she looked me in the eyes, and I yelled, "You'll miss next time." One of my secrets was if I could get a free throw shooter to look at me, and serenely look me in the eyes, I could say some-thing, do something goofy to make them miss, and in the second half, I was going to pull out all the stops to make them miss. At this time, SNU was down 35–31. They started that half 0–2 from the line, but the girl that made the two at the end of the half went to the line and drained two more, putting SNU down eleven points. At the end of the third, SNU seemed to be in a slump; they were behind 52–44.

Then SNU went on a run, taking the lead 54–56 with seven minutes and forty-seven seconds to go in the game. SNU ex-tended their lead to five at one point, but with three minutes forty-one left, SNU only led 61–63. NWOS was shooting free throws, but I stepped up, keeping them from tying the game as they missed one of the two. With two minutes and four seconds to play, SNU and I lost the lead as NWOS sank four free throws in a row, putting SNU down by two.

Soon, there were fifty seconds to go in the game, and it was tied 70–70. NWOS went to the foul line with the score tied at 70–70 with thirty-one seconds to go in the game. They made one of two. Then SNU could take the lead on their next possession. They did, making the score 71–72 with twenty seconds to play. The crowd that had shown up for the end of the game started getting loud as they were chanting defense. Then the controversy started. To this very day, I think NWSO lost the ball out of bounds with five seconds to go, but instead of giving the ball to

SNU, the ref said it was off SNU. NWSO inbounded the ball. Then with one second got a shot off, but it was a miss, as I thought it was over the ref called a foul on SNU leaving .7 seconds on the clock. NWSO was to go to the line to shoot two free throws. SNU took a time out. I yelled so loud that everyone in that stadium heard me when I screamed, "SNU fans, I need you now!"

They were so loud the girl shooting closed her eyes. When she opened them, she looked right at me, missing the first shot. Then the next shot could change the game as a miss meant a win, and a make meant OT. She missed, and I passed out because of how loud I had been. SNU won as she missed. The boys played in the next game. The boy's game was less than exciting; so much so that Baur and I did something that we did not often do. We sat down as the game was being played. The men won 99–79. That night I went to the 405, a restaurant formerly known as Pops. This got me thinking about my grandpa again for a second, but then the two girls in line in front of me turned around. They ended up being Kandyce Freeman and Madeline Schroepfer, and when they looked at me, they both said at the same time, "You're the guy. You know, the guy at the games that gets the crowd into the game." I could tell how their dopamine was coursing through their bodies because I could feel their excitement from that game. It led to a great conversation with two great girls.

The next morning as my nine a.m. class was running late by the usual fifteen minutes, Abby Boyd, the star point guard of the team, walked into class, without her hat on her head for the first time in that class. I knew her dopamine was still hyping her up as she walked over to me. She...banged on my desk...HARD.... She almost broke it. She wanted to tell me thanks for being a great fan.

I soon found out that as I was meandering around campus that my parents were on campus looking all over for me; they wanted to tell me that Pops, my grandfather, died that day at 9:15 a.m.

The next day no one but me showed up for the girls' basketball game, as far as SNU students are concerned. I was poor, to say the least, over the top even for me. I thought that somehow if I was just a better fan, I could help the girls win, but they lost 65–77. I promised myself that I would be a much better fan after that. I was going to mind my Ps and Qs and be a safe fan. I missed the men's game because I went to my room to cry after that game. After Thursday's games, I thought I could magically will the team to win. Now I thought I could be there to cheer on the team. I would love SNU athletics unconditionally and never do anything to hurt them and never miss represent them.

This would be put to the test on Monday, Martin Luther King Jr. Day, January 18th, 2016. That day started with a birthday ordeal for Becca. We took her to Guthrie to a coffee house, and then we went antiquing. It was lots of fun and great. We were bonding even at the part where I almost got eaten by a dog and bought some kids book about horses to give away. The day heated up when I got back to my dorm room because that was when Baur asked me if I wanted to ride with him to Shawnee. He wanted to go to the OBU basketball away game; I was conflicted first because I had missed the women's game, but also because I didn't want to be late for the game. As it turned out, I ended up going with him. We got there so fast we got to see the final score of the girls game. SNU won 81–73. I was so proud of them. Then it was time for the men's game.

At the half of the men's game, SNU was up 52–45 and had lost a lot of momentum at the end of the half. Baur and I decided to go all out in the second half. OBU jumped on SNU, going on a run, tying the game 52–52, but yet their fans were not all that into the game. After a lucky SNU shot, we took the lead 54–52. Then Baur and I started a two-person SNU chant that was so loud it filled the whole arena. We also started making noise when OBU was shooting free throws; they were shooting 50 percent from the line soon. SNU got up 61–54 after OBU missed three three-pointers in a row, but as Baur and I got more in the game, as SNU kept doing better, the OBU fans got more into the game, yelling at the ref. The next missed three-pointer came with a foul, but with Baur and I pumping noise into that place, they missed the first two. Sadly, they sunk the last one because we were not yelling, and we were not yelling because some odd duck of an OBU girl started talking to us. One rule of being a good fan is not talking to opposing fans. She was talking about why we didn't need to be yelling when their team was shooting.

She also told us that we were in their freshman student section. I told her there was no one around us and she couldn't make us leave. Then the next time down the court SNU sent OBU to the line again. Then that goofy, pies for brains of a girl, who probably could not poor crap out of a boot, even with instructions written on the heel of the boot of how to poor out that crap, started trying to talk to me again. She was talking about not talking. So, I yelled at a level that the whole stadium could hear right at her, saying, "Just answer one question: is your mascot bison or bizon?" As I yelled the guy missed the free throw, but then an OBU fat POS of a Barney Fife walked over. He told me at a basketball game that I would have to stop yelling; dumbest thing ever. As OBU started to shoot the next free throw, I yelled, "Sorry but I'm being loud because I left my tickets to the opera in the car so I came to the basketball game." He missed the next free throw. This set the cop off. He grabbed me and dragged me out of the arena. Baur was talking to the cop as he dragged me out. Alan was asking on what grounds he was making me leave. He was also trying to sound legalistic, but as it turned out, he left with me, and the cop never told him anything. We headed back to the dorm. When I got back, the game was over, and it turned out that we gave SNU just enough momentum to win, though I don't remember the score. It was a blowout. The first person I got to tell was a girl. She seemed stunned.

The next day I had a visit from the college chaplain, Mr. Dr.Spindle. He wanted to tell me that he heard about last night and he had seen me as a fan and knew I was not derogatory and thought what I was doing was loving people. Specifically, the athletes at SNU in a great way, and he was willing to do anything that I needed him to do so I could keep going to sporting events. Later that night, I hung out with friends to play a game that I had never played before called murder in the dark. It works like this: First, sift through the cards and remove the jokers, aces, and kings from your deck. Replace one ace and one king in the deck. Shuffle and deal all the cards evenly to each player. The player who has been dealt the ace is the murderer. The player who has been dealt the king is the police officer. Players should keep their cards a secret so that no one knows who the murderer and the policeman are. Turn out the lights in the room. Players should now walk carefully around amongst each other. The murderer will tap other players on the shoulder, silently killing them one by one. The murderer should try and "kill" as many players as they can before the lights go on again. Tapped players can fall or make dramatic dying noises if they want—the more drama, the more fun it is! If players come across someone who has been murdered, they scream out, "Murder in the dark!" The player closest to the lights should turn them on as soon as someone screams. Now the policeman has to figure out who the murderer is from amongst the players still left alive. If they guess the murderer correctly, they win the game. If the police officer is killed, the game is over, so we do not play with a police, just let everyone try and guess who the murderer could be. The murderer should reveal themselves at the end of the game by showing the ace card. I enjoyed it. It was doing this activity that I felt this might be the apostasis of my hero's journey, but truly I had died again in a way having to leave that OBU basketball game, making that my apostasis, or death of laurels, and I felt like I had to be revived. I soon found out what this would take.

CHAPTER SIXTEEN: WATER

"But whoever drinks the water I give them will never thirst. Indeed, the water I give them will become in them a spring of water welling up to eternal life." -John 4:14.

"Life challenges us; it is how we meet these challenges that make us who we are." - Josh George.

On January 22nd, 2016, Baur and I watched the movie *Animal House*. SNU set up a meeting with me about the fact that I had gotten kicked out of the road OBU game. The next day was the meeting. I put on a suit and tie for the meeting. An important person gave me the business but wasn't given the authority to give me a severe punishment. This dean said I had to write a paper on good sportsmanship and was on double-secret probation. Fat, dumb, and stupid might be no way to go through life, but bold, brash, and strategic was a great way to go through life. I thought I was going to be in so much trouble, but the right people seemed to have my back. After I told the dean my story, I think they had my back as well. I thought to myself, *Now I'll truly work on being a better fan of SNU.*

I also started lobbying for a band at sporting events that night as I wrote a seven-page essay on reasons and a need for a band. I was thinking about all the things that SNU athletics needed to change had been. Now we needed a band, then when students came to the football and basketball games, they would get the full college experience. I stayed up all night after watching that movie, writing that essay, and I planned to send it to the dean and other people that might take action. I was there for the Harding Basketball games; the girls lost 60–82, but I pulled out all the stops for the boy's game, and with SNU doing well throughout the boy's game, things were going well. Also, I was recruiting people to be weathermen. The men won 93–87. I then told myself I had to give full effort no matter what. Soon, the men's basketball team was on a winning streak, and the women's team was on a losing streak. They were both slated to play OBU in Bethany. A rematch of the game I had gotten kicked out of earlier that year. I decided to dress up like the revenant and make a sign that said, "Is it Bison or Bizen?" Also, me and the first seven unofficial weathermen started a petition for a band at that game. We got some signatures. I remember one of my friends that signed it telling me later they signed up for the game as the NCAA had approved the band and a placement for them to be in the arena behind the back, just above where I liked to sit it seemed perfect.

The next few days were challenging, but the girls ended their losing streak, beating ECU 57–53. Then baseball beat Arkansas-Monticello 5–4, and tennis lost 0–9. I had been very peaceful at events, but I would soon get somewhat of a break from sports as it was time for a new retreat. It was 2-25-2016 at six p.m. when I got on the bus with John Zehr. There was a lot that Zehr wanted me to be aware of; he was also a big sports fan. I should start doing different types of advertisements for games, like in the school paper; he also reminded me that I had not yet been to a cross-country meet.

We had some great talks about God, life, and girls. We started playing a game called nine square. Zehr wanted to convince us to run for SGA. He made it a point to tell Alan and me. When Baur told me as I went to sleep that I should run, I got to thinking. On the bus, on the way home, Baur told me that his mother wanted him to be on SGA. She had told him this time and again. I did, however, have a chance to win, he thought, but if I didn't want to run, he would run. I told him I still needed time. The next Monday, Baur registered to run for SGA. We decided to launch his campaign after a softball game on March 4th. The softball girls lost both games; they also lost both games the next day. Also, that day our pastor's wife from church told us that she wanted to reboot the after-school program for next year. She just needed Baur or me to be an acting director. Then, in a year, she would take over.

The election was going to be intense, so I did not think that much about the after-school program. Four candidates were running. They were Sam, Baur, Quinn Foster, and another girl. I knew that to win Baur had to win lots of votes from the athletes and the guys that lived in Snowbarger with us as well as the guys that liked going to games, but I knew he would lose votes to Quinn.

One thing we had to do for the campaign was make a video. The truth was, Baur would do anything for SNU sports, including eating a living cockroach (he did) or get shot (he did) or jump off a building (he kind of did). With some movie magic, we made it look like he had done all these things. Then the next part of our campaign was to get ready for a rally-type event that would take place in our school. We also had to clarify our platform and go around the school asking people for their vote. Lots of people wanted to wish us luck on the election and wanted to see what ideas we had for the rally and wanted to know our platform. We even had a visit from the head pastor on campus. Then we told him about our platform. First, we wanted to bring back the weathermen; second, we wanted to start a tradition at basketball games called the Tearing of the Vale. This was going to be similar to the Curtain of Distraction used by Arizona State. Ours would be different because we would act out the Bible loudly to distract free throw shooters, something Baur and I already seemed to be good at.

The next part of our platform was trying to raise awareness for athletics and help them get the right to stack academic scholarships with athletic scholarships. Our last platform idea was to have talks or forums between athletes and nonathletes to help bridge the divide between the two on our campus, and make students want or have more reasons to go to games. Blair S. liked our ideas and told us to print them out so that the students we talked to on rally day would know our plans. We also had the program from when the football team beat OBU. We also had a program where the basketball team beat Harding for the players to sign as they walked into the cafeteria. The day came for the rally. Our booth was close to Quinn's and Sam's; we had one of the best places and I could help direct foot traffic to get them to go to Alan. He was on the side where he could see everyone that came and went from the cafeteria. We also learned that Sam gave a speech to the football players about the importance of them voting for her. I knew we were behind the eight ball, but I didn't know how much. I thought we had a great rally and a good chance to score a two-person runoff with Sam. All we had to do is keep her from winning 50 percent of the vote for the first time. That did not happen. When we got the results, she won without a runoff. I thought it should have been me not Baur. I'm still mad at myself for not running. Also, the next week was hard because SNU's softball team continued their losing streak, losing three games before finally beating Harding to end the streak on Tuesday. They also had an intense thirteen-inning game that we won 10–9 though; there were not lots of fans at those games. One thing that I learned about the softball girls is that they were good at creating their momentum. I wanted to try to learn all their chants so the crowd could chant with them.

I wanted to talk to Baur about what to do next. I wanted to start up the weathermen anyway. I had a plan to get money to start the tearing of the veil. Luckily, I already had a list of people that wanted to be weathermen. I lost that list somewhere, but I think I know who found it. I can get into that a little bit later.

This all went on up until spring break. There was sometimes when I was thinking so much that I could not sleep. Sometimes I would go to the hall closet to use the desk to think and end up falling asleep there. The old saying is, "When life gives you lemons, make lemonade." My saying is "Things are going to happen, good and bad, in life, but if we work hard, in time we can overcome the odds."

A guy who was a big Texas A&M fan wanted to shoot a video talking about the sweet sixteen that week, so as I was losing sleep. I thought it would be a great idea. OU was taking on TAM, and I was a big OU fan. OU would win the game 77–63. The big thing about this show was that it helped me make my list stronger for who should be a weatherman because of the people he told me about. I also needed to hang out with lots of other people. OU played Villanova in the final four; it was a rematch, and OU won the first game by a wide margin. Now there is a new record for the biggest final four blowout. Nova won 95–51. I had never been drunk, and I've never been drunk after that night. After that game, I looked for some beers. I had six, and I drank all of them. In college, drinking will play a factor of some kind. As easy as it is to say go to a school that has a no drinking policy like SNU, and one that I had broken. I will say that no matter where you go, the opportunity for drinking will come up. What you do is your choice, but remember that drinking can change how you participate. If you do want to drink in college, do it safely, and never plan on getting drunk; knowing your limit is important. Getting drunk will not solve any problems; having good friends and talking solves and helps with lots. Kyler Ross came by just before I started drinking. He wanted to throw all the beer out. I told him that by the end of the night, they would all be gone. Kyler told me if I were to drink anything I should stay in the room to avoid trouble. After I finished my fifth beer I was ready to go to sleep, when I got a text from someone who wanted to play volleyball. I couldn't resist.

I told myself I would not get into trouble. It is important to know that my wallet is brown and Ory's wallet is dark black. We played six games, and I was all over the place. I played one of my best games ever, but I had to go to the bathroom and needed to leave and grabbed Ory's wallet on my way back to my dorm. Luckily, someone let me in to the dorm. Then Ory knocked on the door. He had my wallet. He also knew I had his we traded wallets and he left.

The next morning, I had the only hangover I ever had, and Baur left to drive to Kansas. I had to think about who I could trust to tell them about last night and convince them to drive me to get breakfast at Taco Bell. I thought of Nathan Black. Let's just say I truly trusted his character more than anyone on the floor for this mission. In my hangover, I made him an unofficial weatherman for next year. Later that year, he joined the flag runners so he could go to more games and support SNU athletics the way he felt best, and I was proud of him for that. I also learned another college lesson. Do not get drunk. I had loads of fun in college and never needed to be drunk for any of them.

Next, on the 4th of April was the day of the other election. Colin Pasque won his election, and Quinn Foster won his election. It looked like Sam had two good guys on her team that I trusted to help me make the unofficial weathermen a little more official. Then the 13th of April was the day of the last sporting event I went to for that semester. I went to two softball games, both home games and both against OBU. I tried to write down the individual sayings that our dugout was using, and I was also a super fan that day. After the first game, Sam looked at me and gave me a big thumbs up as SNU had won 2–0 the next game. I got louder and felt I did even better. I also really hoped that this meant the weathermen would happen next semester. SNU won 7–1. The one run OBU scored was my fault. I was doing a "Hey batter, swing batter" chant and accidentally helped her time it up perfectly.

After that game, I got a call from my college pastor. He knew I had been applying for jobs. and he had a friend that he knew from a church he used to be a part of; he had gotten me an interview with this person. The interview was with a guy named Blake from Shiloh camp, and he was very interested in hiring me and wanted me to join the team and be a camp counselor for that summer. The next day I got the job and a new phone, as well as three As on the major end-of-the-year tests. Life seemed to be progressing, and SNU athletics was kind of on hold, but not for long as life went on.

May the 1st was big. I was going to be part of a small open mic night; the boys, mainly Jase Bagwell and Josh Oliver, told me that I had to do the open mic night using my poetry talent because I might meet some great people.

Soon, it was draft day; time to pick a dorm room, and Baur as usual did not want to go with me to pick where to live next year. I got the best dorm in the school in the Chapman apartments. I did however tell Baur we were back in Snow. That lasted seven seconds, but the look on his face was so mad.

Then on the 7th of the month, I took my next final and went to the end-of-the-year banquet, where they were giving out a gift card for SNU's number-one fan. This would be judged by so many social media posts, but I was not posting to social media when I was at games. I was cheering on SNU. Needless to say I did not win; some girl won. She was at lots of games but not a better fan than me. I sent an email to Foster about how this fan award needed to be about attendance and how loud you were or how good of a fan you were, not social media. He said if it was that way, I would have won, and he thought I should have won, but it was time for summer. I would be back next year and next year to help SNU athletics and did not think I would win that award knowing it was likely not going to change. I set some new goals. One, win that sports award if possible, without too many posts on social media; two, join and be a part of the gender equality club; and three, let God take me in what direction that God wanted me to go. God and goals are a good place to be in college. Setting goals and having a to do list as well as a list of hopes and dreams is very important. That can lead you to taking who you are inside and showing it to everyone allowing you to live your life as you are.

CHAPTER SEVENTEEN: PLACE OF PEACE

"So God was kind to the midwives and the people increased and became even more numerous." -Exodus 1:20.

Summers had tended to be hard for me, but that began to change the summer of 2016. 5-24-16: I started rope training with some staff at Shiloh. Some people just wanted to have a belay certification. That week brought about challenges, and one thing that I need to say is that I have a fear of heights. Doing rope course training and learning how to climb and belay was hard for me because of dealing with the heights. I also had to learn new types of knots; they were similar to ones that I knew from earning my Eagle Scout, but just a little different. That week I learned the importance of overcoming fears. Every day that week I woke up dreading the challenge of the next day, but there were several parts I enjoyed, like planning lessons from the ground or learning group games such as Perfect SquareTime. It worked like this: it was about 15–30 minutes. To do this you need –five to twenty people and a long piece of rope tied together and a blindfold for each person. The rules are this: First, have your coworkers stand in a circle holding a piece of the rope. Then instruct everyone to put on their blindfold and set the rope on the floor. Have everyone walk a short distance away from the circle. Next, ask everyone to come back and try to form a square with the rope without removing their blindfolds. Set a time limit to make it more competitive. To make it even more difficult, instruct some team members to stay silent.

The objective is focused on strong communication and leadership skills. By instructing some team members to be silent, this game also requires an element of trust across the team, allowing team members to guide each other in the right direction. Things like this were fun, but the next week was super fun.

I got a new Bible from Shiloh camp. The reason for this is that they had highlighted verses that they wanted us to share with the kids. Most of these kids were inner-city and most had very little knowledge about God or Jesus. The lesson showed us how to talk to kids that never knew anything about God. We were teaching what Shiloh called the God story and what it was all about. I enjoyed getting to know the counselors, a Jake, a Matt a Dustin, a Kait, an Isabella, a Meg, a Lauren, and Justus Hill who was an SNU basketball commit for next year. The counselors had good relations and it really developed over that week. We also learned what the weekly routine would be. The kids would show up at eight a.m. every day, and we should show up at 7:15 a.m. every day. I showed up at around 6:60 to 7:00, being one of the first ones there. Next would be the intro service to introduce the theme for the day. Then kids would have time to memorize the day's verse and learn about God.

This is when the kids asked lots of questions, and they got good at learning the verses because they realized that they could get points, and the boys' and girls' teams with the most points won a medal at the end of the week. Next, there was a morning event. Then they had lesson two, and then lunch, where we gave out bumblebees, and then two more events before free time. I was always assigned to belay for free time. If a kid accepted Christ in his life, they got to ring the bell. I had a hard group, but they had the competitiveness that we won every game with. I had a boys' group, five, and we beat boys group four every time except the last one on Friday.

Friday was a special night. It was show night. The night parents got to see the verses that the kids had learned. There was a talent time, where the kids performed poems, art, and drama/dancing. There were also awards given out as well, including Heart, for the student that showed love to other campers; the hype, to the hypest camper; the leadership to a major camp leader; but the best award to get was the Heisman of the camp. This award was called the Good Samaritan award. We also had to make Character Qualities, where we picked two to four qualities that were seen in kids and wrote one sentence about how they embodied that. They were not always true; sometimes they were what we wanted to see in a kid. Sometimes in life we have to look into ourselves and see what we want to see in us and others and use encouragement to bring those things out.

The best moment of that first week was Wednesday, when my hardest kid asked me to help him to ask Jesus into his heart. I remember that. Mostly I remember after that he went from my hardest kid to my best kid. After that, I took a long drive through the neighborhoods around the camp. It looked bad, so to speak; many of the homes had missing shingles on their roofs. There was graffiti and lots of bus stops with advertisements on them. It also seemed similar to the area around my college church. I learned that families living in poverty experience several barriers to receiving treatment and accessing mental health services. One of the primary barriers is the lack of health insurance, which prevents families from being able to afford treatment. There is also a limited number of mental health providers under managed care plans, making it harder to access treatment at reduced costs.

Also, most of the kids only had one working parent; usually, the other one was in a gang, on drugs/recovery, or had been in prison and could not get a job. Many parents were low income because lots did not have any college education. I felt some dropped out of college. This led to the kids loving being part of the camp because they loved how we cared for them. They had trouble understanding God. Love and unconditional love were hard for them as well as something they had no experience with. Most parents focused more on making ends meet and less on their kids. Doing goofy cheers, learning how to tie a tie, hearing Stephen Moore talk. This all took the kids away from that life and put them in a place to fall in love with Jesus, because his love through us was some of the first love that they ever experienced.

Week two was a great week because of how many times the bell rang as it rang twenty-three times. Yet it had lots of hard times. The thing that we did to get through the hard times was Blinde Barnabas. Leaving notes to someone that did not know we were sending them, a note about how well they were doing or a small blessing. After five weeks, we had turned that camp into a place of peace. Life can always have something new; it's not about what happens to you but doing the next right thing. Helping others and praying for them can go a long way.

CHAPTER EIGHTEEN: BE POSITIVE AND HAVE FRIENDS

8-22-16: Baur and I moved into our apartment. The next day, as I was walking around on the balcony of our apartment, John C., one of the football players, came up to me and asked if I wanted to join the storm chasers. Sam was making the weathermen but changed the name. It turned out that everyone that I had put on that list for possible weathermen had been contacted by Sam to join the club. It was a great group of people. Sam gave us the expectations for the group. She told us that we would have monthly meetings with a signup sheet for events. Some people at the meeting talked about cheer coordination or theme nights for games. We also talked about other athletic issues on campus.

The next night I was eating in Whataburger with some people from improv. Joining clubs is very important in college. It can help to blow off steam and put people around that can be helpful. Improv was a club I was in that always kept me on my toes. It helped me to be creative along with giving me a time to let lose. Having a time to let loose with others is so important. One way to find clubs is to ask around, or if someone ask you to join a club, what I would do is ask to visit for one meeting, then see if the club passes the test, fitting you, giving you a chance to let loose. Improv did that more me big time. I could be goofy doing skits like games, and then we would go out to eat, and we could talk about life and get some counseling from those around us.

One night that came after a great improv club, something that Jase had recruited me to join. Being part of improv was a great place to talk about SNU athletics, meet interesting people, and get ideas about how to distract opposing teams. I liked being a part of this because it was a great stress reliever, and anyone in college needs an outlet for that. That night I learned two things about my college church. First, I had become the after-school program director, and it lasted about two weeks before they told me that there was no funding and they were permanently discontinuing the program. At that point, I had recruited the people I needed to volunteer every day and had lesson plans and a daily schedule, and I also had made contact with lots of parents. I was hurt, and SNU athletics quickly became the main focus for this semester.

The 2nd of September was the first test of the newly formed storm chasers as SNU had a big home soccer game. The big thing from that night that was positive is the soccer team seemed to like getting some applause as they left the pitch. The storm chasers were instrumental in starting that applause. Life is going to happen; things outside of sports and friends are going to change who you are. Baur and I faced some challenges that week; every week is going to have some challenges. The best way to prepare is to be positive. If SNU lost or if there was a night where improv was hard or school was overwhelming, putting into practice a positive attitude was important for me.

In fact, I wrote it down in one of my notebooks that anytime I was not being positive to take a mental note and change my mind set.

There were break ups and babysitting that week that made it a very hard week. School and having four tests in one week made it very hard as well. Soon, September 20th, I had a volleyball game that I could go to where the storm chasers proved to be super loud and a great help to the team as SNU won in four sets. On the 22nd, the soccer teams faced off with Ouachita Baptist. The women played their hearts out but lost 2–0. The men's game had another great Josh George moment. Before the games, I had watched a soccer movie to get ready. It was the original *Fever Pitch*, and in that film, one of the guys gets behind the goal to create a distraction during a penalty kick.

I tried to do that but did not do a good job because they still made the goal, and I was told that no one was allowed to do that, and I could get kicked out of the game for trying a stunt like that. As it turns out, SNU ended up winning 3–1. That moment seemed to turn the game around. It was after that game two girls and four guy storm chasers stopped me in my car to ask about how we could do better next time and to give me a vuvuzela for next time. The vuvuzela was something that Sam had gotten for all the storm chasers. On the 28th of September, we had our first monthly meeting. I just used the nickname my high school football coach gave me. I went over to Nathan Black's dorm that night just to tell him about my frustrations. Being part of improv and having others that could help me keep a positive attituded was important. There is a well-known saying that life is hard. It is very hard, and we can never be perfect, but having accountability can help us be better. I often would walk randomly into rooms looking for accountability. People did not always say what I wanted to hear, but they usually said what I needed to hear, and I could do the same for them. This help to stay positive and do what needed to be done.

The thing was one of his sweet mates nicknamed me Kramer because of how I would walk in randomly for random things, and the truth was I had been doing the Kramer thing all of my college life. I did it to everyone. I thought I should have put Kramer as my nickname because I was the Kramer of SNU. Life still went on. On the 29th, SNU played ECU in volleyball. This game I will always remember as a great game. Every time their short number fifteen got up to serve, we would start chanting "Net!" It was six times she hit the ball into the net. She started getting subbed out every time she came up to serve. They needed her in the game because she was their best setter on the team; this fact led SNU to win 3–0.

Then the women's soccer team got to go up against ECU, and one of the ECU moms recognized me from the volleyball game on the 29th just two days ago. It did not stop me from being the best fan I could be. I was great, and SNU played great, winning 4–1. I screamed a goal for around a minute after that fourth goal. The ECU moms left the game as SNU ramped it up, and the storm chasers put a bow on the game with an "I Believe" chant. Football also beat Arkansas-Monticello 31–17 on October 8th. One of my favorite nights with friends was when I went to Tanner Wilson's place to hang with him and Nathan Black. We just watched some not super funny YouTube videos. One was of some fat woman eating, but it was the simplicity of these times that made college great. I could go to just about anyone's room and walk in and they would welcome me and we could talk about anything in life, whether it seemed dumb or great! One of my favorite nights was when Baur and I were invited to a girl's birthday party on the 17th of October. Taylor was her name. She met us one night and gave me her number and texted me to be at her party. Most people left, and it was just Baur and I with her and her roommate Rose. The truth is that by keeping a positive attitude, people seemed to be more willing to be around me, and I enjoyed being around others more.

SNU had a volleyball game that was my favorite of the year. I got their captain benched after the end of the first set. She started playing badly after I got into her head. Before the game, I asked her for her number. Then I tried to talk to her from the stands. She looked up at me twice and missed two serves. After that, she was benched. I remember bragging the next day at breakfast. I bragged about my success at that game. I said I would never forget the name of the girl that I got benched that night. The truth is, I only know it starts with an L.

On my birthday that year, I spent it with my friends, and we had become lots like a family, and school plus the SNU athletics work that I had been doing had become my business. Two days later, I built an altar in my room and started cutting time out to pray. When working at Shiloh, I had learned how to be in constant prayer. Then I told myself that I would be in prayer all the time. That lasted all of ten minutes. I did however take out my Bible and start reading for one minute, then I realized that to further my faith I had to learn about God, be in a relationship with God, and help others. Then I prayed about many of my friends. There is power in prayer like there is the power in knowing others have your back and you have their backs. College goes by so fast; that is why I would take the time just to look around the table and take joy that we were all together, knowing that the time for that was running out.

CHAPTER NINETEEN: JOY

"And there were in the same country shepherds abiding in the field, keeping watch over their flock by night. And, lo, the angel of the Lord came upon them, and the glory of the Lord shone round about them: and they were sore afraid. And the angel said unto them, Fear not: for, behold, I bring you good tidings of great joy, which shall be to all people. For unto you is born this day in the city of David a Saviour, which is Christ the Lord." -Luke 2: 8–14

On October 27th, SNU won both at women's soccer and volleyball. To tell you the truth, I do not remember much about that night except for, afterwards, I was happy. Just because we are being positive or someone is positive does not mean that they are happy. A preacher in a sermon talked about how anytime that we are asked how we are we almost always say something like "I'm good," or "Okay." We keep our lives simple and to the point unless we are with close friends. Baur said that he would go with me to any sporting event if I would go climb Mount Everest with him. That was not going to happen. I might have been willing to go to the Wichita Wildlife Refuge in Holy City, Oklahoma. In life, it is important to make compromises. Happiness is H=S+C+V; happiness is the factors under one's voluntary control plus life circumstances. Trying to make yourself and others happy can be impossible, but listening and trying to help with life's circumstances is important and how friendships grow.

At this time in college, I wanted to get closer to some of the guys in Hills.

I ended up leaving a party to go to a men's soccer game. They beat Mary (ND) 3–1. I was not loud and not very into the game. Life got grim that night, and I seemed to stay grim until the 9th of November. That day was when I found out that I had gotten a new room. Now all I had to do was some paperwork. Soon, room 303 in Hills would be mine. That is when all the friends I had were very important, as they helped me make the final arrangements.

The next day was more exciting as the volleyball team faced OBU. The composite score was 35–10 in favor of SNU. We were up by two sets. I think almost all the storm chasers had shown up at that point in the game, and the stadium was a ruckus. Lexie Matthews got the third set off on the right foot with an SNU point. That led the crowd to start rubbing their hands together and being silent as we served, but we lost the next two points. Then we did an ABC cheer to count the number of hits on the ball. SNU snagged another point, leading to a small cheer, but we were unusually silenced as OBU got two more points. Then one of the storm chasers said, "Let's get loud." Next, we helped SNU win the next three points, making that set 5–4 in favor of SNU. Soon, an error by Courtney Bowie put OBU up 9–7.

It was time to let the team know it was going to be okay and we were going to retake control. I started my favorite SNU chant, and Kaitlyn Vought, one of my favorite players, looked back at me and up into the crowd just before the ball was served she would win the next point for SNU. Then Bowie made up for her mistake by winning a point to tie the set 9–9. After that, SNU took the lead and held it, but then OBU made a massive sub as they were only behind by one with the score 16–17. We got louder than we had been all night. SNU won two more points, taking a 16–19 lead. Then OBU took a timeout, and we were inflamed with joy. Soon, an "I Believe" chant rose from the crowd. OBU had a cool play, leading them to win the next point, but I did not think they were going to come back. Yet soon the score was 25–25 in a scenario where the next two points would win the set and for SNU winning the set would mean winning the game. That "I Believe" chant came back, and the crowd started hugging each other as Bailee Turang and Courtney Bowie each won a point for SNU, winning the set, and the game was amazing.

That was Thursday of what Sam had branded as our "away going" week. Because the football team had an away game at OBU, the week was called "away going." Sam did a good thing, as she spent time renting busses and making a way to go as a big group. Students could buy a package that got them a shirt, a seat on the bus, and a ticket to the game. Ultimately, she did a great job with the week the night after the volleyball game. There was a big party that I think she planned.

Friday night, SNU had a men's and women's basketball game. The men had two games that week as they would play on Saturday also. If the bus ran fast, I could go to Shawnee to the OBU football game and make all three basketball games that week. Game one, the women won 80–68, but the men's game was closer than that. Having a full crowed at events seemed awesome. The next morning, I got up to get on the bus.

This game would be another off-the-wall game as the bus got there just in time. People were joking with me about the time that I got kicked out of the basketball game. SNU started the game having a two-minute-and-twenty-two-second drive and getting a touchdown, taking an early 7–0 lead. OBU then made it clear that their strategy was to run the clock, as they put together a drive over five minutes and got a field goal. The chant war between the two student sections got big during the next four drives. It was a quarter of punting. That is until there was one minute and twenty-seven seconds left in the quarter. SNU ended the quarter as it had started it, with a big TD, taking a 14–3 lead. Our team and crowd took a huge advantage. Over the next quarter, we were way louder than them. People joked with me about getting too loud even though I was far away from saying anything negative. OBU's run game finally found a hole. They got a seventy-three-yard burst to end the half.

The score was 14–10. The crowd started the second half off right with my favorite SNU chant and we made it loud. Leading to multiple OBU false starts on that first drive. This helped us take back the momentum. We scored again but missed the extra point, making the score 20–10. Our D stepped up; we ran the ball okay, and they ran the ball okay. They seemed to accept the loss. The rest of the game went by fast. I looked at my watch to see if we would be back at SNU for the basketball game. The football team had beaten OBU 20–10.

Everyone that was at the football game just about went to the basketball game. The score seemed close, but SNU seemed to dominate. SNU won 91–87. Deshon Portley scored twenty-six points, and the crowd even chanted his name at one point. Then we all went to dinner together. It made for a great day of sports. Something also important to keep in mind that we talked about at dinner is if you're a Christian, it's important to love. That group of people had done so to each other that day by simply hanging out with each other and working hard for something bigger than themselves. They had done something for the betterment of their school, our school.

That would be handy when one of our lesser rivals started sending us negative messages on social media. The messages started being sent on December the 1st. We did not have a game with them until the 6th of December. The messages were from OC. They were a school in Edmond known as Oklahoma Christian. They had gotten some of our storm chasers on social media, and they told us how bad we were going to lose to them. They did have lots of fans show up at that game, and they were outlandish. They did make it seem as if these games were rivalry games, but the scores did not reflect that at all. Our men's team won 81–60, and our women's team won 81–65. Both basketball games went well. Also, in December, some of the boys took a trip up to Pikes Peak, which made for a great story.

I wanted to have a semester of all As. I had just taken a midnight study break to go get some donuts from the Krispy Kreme dumpster. We both knew that they threw unopened boxes of donuts away at the end of the week. After waiting two hours in a parked car, I found out this was true. Baur and I had been invited to watch *Star Wars* with some friends and were going to take them donuts. One of the guy's girlfriends had gotten pizza for us, and life seemed great, but it got even better. Jase started to talk about wanting to go to the Grand Canyon. We all wanted to go on a big trip. Soon, it was 10:30 p.m. and someone said, "Let's just start the movie." Then some of us got into two cars and started driving to Pikes Peak, because it was closer to us and maybe just as cool as the Grand Canyon.

We had donuts and pizza and a thirteen-hour drive. I took shotgun for the first three hours but started to fall asleep, so the other guys moved me to the back seat. As I woke up, I got to see a Colorado sunset. We had all these plans, but as we started heading up the mountain, it started to snow. One of the cars we took started having problems. The park was closing. Ice started to fall, and the roads were getting bad. It doesn't sound like much, but after a snowball fight, a run up the mountain, an odd talk in a gift store, and a football game, we ended up having a blast. Doing something ridiculous and spontaneous has a way of bringing the character out of others. That's exactly what that trip was. The "say yes" attitude I had adopted might have been paying off. Even when something happened to that was obscure.

I ended up talking with Britt Dawson about the crazy end to the semester. After that moment, I moved my stuff out into my car to get ready for the move. Though I spent the last day of that semester living out of my car. Even though I did not have a final, I still got my time with almost everyone I wanted to. Taking the time out to talk to others is so important right before you leave; it brings a type of peace, and you can share memories and hopes. It is the memories and hopes that turn into joy. Joy is a major part of life. Joy can lead us to grace, and to the people that God has made us to become.

CHAPTER TWENTY: EXPERIENCE

"I have fought the good fight, I have finished the race, I have kept the faith." -2 Timothy 4:7

Life changes rapidly. There are good years and bad years. In college, there are good semesters and bad semesters. Going into the semester, it felt like one of my last chances to help SNU. I knew I had to take an extra semester to teach. So, this semester felt extra important.

The semester had its first big moment on January 16th, 2017. That was the date of the SNU and OBU basketball games in Bethany, Oklahoma. I was determined that SNU would beat both teams. Even though I was living alone, I managed to have room for what I needed to take to SNU basketball games. I had gotten a new red suit and a Redman suit for Christmas and would go on to use them both lots at SNU sporting events. As for that night,

I chose the Redman suit. Also, over Christmas break, I had a scheduling crisis. I had found myself in a Thursday night class and had to get out of it because SNU had too many games on Thursdays. I was in a Western US history class, but I replaced it with a Russian history class. Luckily, I knew the professor and ended up having lots of friends in that class.

All of this had led up to the start of a great semester, and it was the night of January 16th that started it all. The girls took the court. It seemed like no time at all had passed when the final buzzer sounded. I knew SNU had won. We had been playing a great game, then I looked up at the scoreboard to see SNU won 96–65. The men followed suit winning 88–57. SNU's basketball teams started great home winning streaks. Between the two teams, there were four basketball games the next week. They started on the 26th as SNU played Ouachita. SNU won both games. The women won 90–62, and the men won 84–78. Then on that Saturday, the 28th, Henderson State got the brunt of me and the SNU basketball teams. Our women's team won 84–72, and the men won 81–57.

These games were great! When I would walk in the stadium, the old alumni fans would greet me and thank me for my support and attendance. Professors would ask me how or why I had become such a big SNU fan. Athletes started eating with me in the cafeteria. There was even some freshman that started taking Josh George statistics. The way the statistics worked was, every time

SNU's opponent missed a free throw that was a block, if SNU got a steal because of me, that was a transition credited to me, then if SNU got an open three because of how loud the crowd was, then that was a JG 3. I loved talking to these freshmen after games and listening to them tell me how I did running the student section.

Then next Tuesday, January 31st, the SGA was putting on a night of capture the flag. I remembered how much fun I had doing this before and hoped to have another great game. This time I was told that I would be trying to capture the other team's flag, not playing defense. I was on the blue team trying to get the green team's flag. I found myself walking along the neutral zone. I was walking up and down, trying to find an opening. At this point, I was in a cluster of people and had an idea of how to get away. Soon, everyone was walking in the same direction, and I started walking slower and did an about-face. I looked behind me to see this short little, tiny girl was following me. Her name was Lauren Toney. She told me she was a track and cross-country runner and that I needed to be careful if I tried to run. I did try, and she caught me. We talked about the opening of the new baseball stadium that would happen later that week.

Not long after that, SNU's baseball stadium had its grand opening on February the 3rd. I was there, and it was a cool stadium. The team lost both games that day. I had fun and enjoyed them the best I could. It was not about the game it was about the fact that SNU was paying attention to their athletics. As life on campus got better, I was asked to do a Who's the Man interview. This was an event that SNU put on that was like a Miss America for guys. Two guys from each class were picked using the interviews. This was kind of a big deal. I prepared for the interview by reviewing who I was. I was a big part of SNU athletics, I was a poet and in improv club, and I was part of a prayer team. The first question asked in most interviews is, "Tell us a little bit about yourself," but that was not the case for this interview.

I had done lots of prep work for the interview, and it would be the oddest interview I would ever have. I was asked to propose to someone in the room. It was odd. I was asked to sing a Disney song. I was asked why I should be a part of this. It was crazy. However, that night ended on a high note as Nathan Black and Tanner Willson were making a mini film for SNU's small film festival and came up to me asking if I would be a part of their idea. They told me that Tanner was interviewing for Who's the Man to be one of the two juniors. The next night, we got to work writing a script. It ended up being a lawman's tail. The names of the characters were all named after the holidays. There was Hanukkah, whose opening line was "Shalom." We also used the names Kwanza and Christmas. The villain was Crampus, and he had killed my character's wife, who we named Easter. I was named Kwanza. We had a great script, but it wasn't meant to be. On the 9th of February, SNU won two more home basketball games; the women won 81–67, the men won 85–59.

It was February 13th, and it was the night that I had to pick a walk-up song for Who's the Man. I had asked lots of people what song was best. The one I felt best about and took was "Hips Don't Lie" by Shakira. I felt this was important if I had any chance of winning. As I was thinking about this, Tanner and Nathan started knocking on my door loudly. Tanner had picked some songs for his walk-up song, and his band was going to carry him on stage. I needed an escort for Who's the Man.

I went over to Nathan Blacks and asked him what to do. Soon, he had bought a giant teddy bear. The plan was that I would dress up as the bear, and using a Bluetooth earwig, Nathan would tell me where to go, as I could not see in the suit. I would then walk up to all the girls around campus.

I got into the suit, and to tell the truth, everyone said I looked a little like Pooh Bear. We walked up to a girl who giggled big and knew immediately that it was me. As I was dancing on a chair, Tyler Stark put me on his shoulder and carried me outside. All in all, it was a great prank. I freaked some people out. I learned none of the girls really seemed to notice. In life, you're going to have the opportunity to do goofy things; if you do them well, it'll be worth it. A girl wanted to play cards with some of the people that were in the lobby of the dorm.

I had an idea to make an event at a basketball game. I got the idea on the 16th of February as I went to both of SNU's basketball games. I thought about an event in high school that was called "Single or Not." If a person was single, they had to wear a green shirt to the event; if they were not, they would put on a red shirt, but if they did not know, they could put on a yellow shirt. Unfortunately, green and yellow are not in SNU's color wheel. So, this was the plan: grey shirts would be single, white would be I don't know, and red would be not single. Now how to get this event around the school, and how to do it anonymously. I remembered that Nathan Black had created an email called the SNU Activities Email. It was a fake email not sanctioned by SNU or the SGA.

He made it three years ago and only sent an email to Tyler Stark to try to get him to get a fake free snow cone so he could get him out in the game wet bandits, an assassination game where the winner was the last person standing; people got a target and did not know who had them as a target, and people got out by getting started with a water gun.

Now I would use that email to reach every girl on campus. The way I did this was by taking the names off the emails sent to the dorms on campus by the RDs of the dorms. I had one from two of the dorms and got a female friend of mine to forward an email to me from Bracken, so I had a list of every girl on campus. I had a list of almost every guy. I did not have the ones that lived in Snow at the time. There were some almost immediate problems: First, I did not do a spelling check. Next, I got with Tanner, Nathan, Marshal Jones, and Noah. We walked all over campus talking about what to do next. Two girls on the SGA had gotten into a mini fight over the origin of this email.

To counteract, we wrote a new email and put out posters advertising the event. This email was short and to the point, as it turned out the majority of campus loved the idea and showed up to the game. It was kind of a singles' mixer. SNU won both games, the first 87–69, and the second 68–64. I had lots of fun.

The next weekend was also an important one, at least on that Friday and Saturday, March the 3rd and 4th. On that Friday I had a group of people take a ride up to Bartlesville to support the men's basketball team in the conference tournament. If they won the first game, they were major favorites, so I chose not to go. It ended up being a mistake as they lost 63–74. That night there was an unofficial storm chaser meeting. We talked about expectations for next year and if there was a way we could learn the softball cheers for each batter. At that moment, we all knew that I looked at the returning production for SNU's men's basketball team and knew we would be really good next year and we would likely win the conference next year.

That Saturday, because I was not going to a basketball game, it made it the perfect day to film my video for Who's the Man. I had a song that would be the song for the video, and that was Blondie's "Heart of Glass." The video plan was to film me breaking glass and flying a kite, but it was much too windy to fly a kite. I ended up playing pool against Nathan and coming back to win;

I also broke lots of glass and shook my butt some along with dancing on a car. It ended up being a hit, but Tanner's video was also good, and I thought Seth's video would be amazing, as he was super creative and known to be musical. The softball home opener was also that afternoon, and SNU lost 0–8. There were several storm chasers at the game, but it was clear we had to get better. As the game got worse, people started asking me about *Who's the Man*, trying to give me advice.

March was a much more routine month, going to softball games and as many SNU sporting events as I could, preparing my Who's the Man show. I worked on my poetry, my walk-up, my improv. One thing I loved about going to improv club is that afterward, we would go to Whataburger and Jase would give me pointers. One of the most interesting moments in March was when I got really mad at myself for not executing the walk up the way I wanted to, and I started cursing at myself. Greg knocked on my door and gave me some good consultants. Still, it was April 1st, and softball had a big game against Southwestern Oklahoma State; SNU ended up winning 15–7. Soon, the craziness would pick back up in the middle of April. The storm chasers had a huge turnout for both baseball and softball games. It was a double senior night, making them great events as they ended up being the last two SNU home games of the semester.

The next weekend after the senior nights on April 17th, things started speeding up. That night I had to jump in a lake twice. Lake Overholser. Needless to say it was cold. The event started when Christan Leesburg started playing his vuvuzela loudly. So loud that many people in the hall came out of their rooms to see what was happening. My mind went back to times living in Snowbarger when something would happen spontaneously and we did not know what it was, but we knew it would be fun. I asked Leesburg what all the noise was about, and he told me that people were going to jump into the lake. A group of my friends had placed a bet on every game of the Memphis Grizzlies and the San Antonio Spurs NBA playoff seven-game series. The Spurs had won the first two games, so I chose the Grizzlies, and that's the side that Jase was on. However, because we had lost two games, we had to jump into the lake twice.

I had to put that bet into the back of my mind because the night of game three was the night before Who's the Man. Luckily, Memphis won because I spent the night practicing. The memories kind of a blur. I changed outfits four times. My hips don't lie. Walk up went great; I had a great improv and a great act. I did not sleep at all that night. In college, that doesn't always seem to be a reason for everything. Just going with it sometimes is important, just having faith that even if something doesn't have a rhyme or reason it may.

I thought about all I had been a part of on campus and realized that, in truth, it could not have happened without God or my friends. God's glory gives us a chance to live. It is God's glory that he made this world. Then people disobeyed God. This disobedience led to a separation of people and God. With the grace of God, we can accept Christ. Christ died for our sins, taking on that separation, allowing us to truly experience God living in all of us. Knowing this will lead to us experiencing God as well as experiencing God's world. I knew this and thanked God for all my college experience. Then as I was leaving breakfast to finally get some rest, Kristian Stitt grabbed my arm and said, "Hey, you've got to be at the end of the year Storm Sports Awards." I told him I would be there.

The next week ended up being crazy. I found myself pushing a grocery cart around campus and vehemently throwing it to the second floor of a girl's dorm. That night I watched Memphis beat the Spurs in the overtime Thriller that was game four, then I watched several guys jump in Lake Overholser. The next night I took the Blazin' Challenge and failed at Buffalo Wild Wings. Life seemed to be getting back to normal. I did have to jump into the lake after Memphis lost another game. I was sure that they're going to lose game six in Memphis. I went to class that day and I couldn't wait for the Storm Sports Awards that would take place in two days. Even though I knew it wouldn't be much. Then I was heading up to the cafeteria, when the crazy got big time.

Jase Bagwell walked up to me and said, "Hey, you got thirty bucks?" Then he said, "There are thirty-dollar seats for the Memphis Spurs game, and some of us have already bought the tickets. Let's go to the library and we'll use your card to buy tickets, and we'll be leaving for the game in about thirty minutes." Well, I spent thirty dollars. I got the tickets, and lo and behold I got in a car headed for a six-hour-and-fifty-seven-minute car ride to Memphis, Tennessee, from Bethany, Oklahoma. Jonathan Perez and Easton ended up going to the game with us. After the drive, we got parked. The game clock read seven minutes and twenty second minutes until tip-off. I finally got to my seat. I asked Jonathan Perez if he would take a picture. It is still on social media. It is of me at this game today, and I still keep the towel that I got from the game. The towel read, "We don't bluff." If Memphis lost, it would mean another jump in the lake.

The game was close going into the fourth quarter as the Spurs led 75–74. Then Jace leaned over to me and said, "I feel like the dress has taken the Spur's best punch." We. Will. Win. It didn't seem long, but then soon, fans were on their feet clapping as the Spurs were dribbling the game out. Memphis season was ending. They were clapping to show appreciation for the efforts that their team had given for the city that season. I was proud of those fans. It was something cool to see and be a part of and have in my memory.

We got back early Friday morning, even got back in time for Friday classes. I remember at lunch people were coming up and talking to us saying, "Wait, is this real? How is the post real? You were in Memphis last night?" We also had to jump in the lake. Most of that Friday I thought about Saturday and the Storm

Sports Awards. That night I agreed to jump in the lake after the sports awards.

April 29th, 2017: The first-ever Josh George award was given to me, Josh George. It was an award that the SGA had recommended to the athletics director to be created in my honor and given out every single year. It was for SNU's most enthusiastic fan each year. Samantha Quinn Foster and Pasque had recommended it. That night's MC described the award's history, my character and who I was. Then he called my name to receive the award. Pasque met me on stage. He would go on to win several awards that night, but ended up giving that award out to me. Needless to say my legacy at SNU was secure. That semester ended up on a high note. I ended up running from Yukon to Bethany because of a bet, but what are shenanigans, I thought. Most of them seemed pretty insignificant because nothing measured up like that night of the award.

Honestly, it didn't hurt all that bad because I knew I had the award and I knew that I was coming back for one more semester and I have a chance to continue with SNU Athletics. My Mom told everyone she knew about my award. I feel like I heard that almost all summer. My dad was impressed that I took him to see it. It had been placed in the basketball arena by the end of that summer. Ultimately, what that award meant to me was like what the medals meant to Han and Luke and Chewie at the end of New Hope.

CHAPTER TWENTY-ONE: ENDING

"And when thou hast stayed three days, then thou shalt go down quickly and come to the place where thou didst hide thyself when the business was in hand, and shalt remain by the stone Ezel." -1 Samuel 20:19.

After another long summer, it was time to go back to school, but I wasn't moving into a college dorm room. I was going to live at home for the first half of the semester and in Yukon for the second half. I would live with a person I had met last semester, the second half of the semester. I was going to be a student-teacher in both Yukon and in Norman at Alcott Middle School. I had set up these living situations. If I needed to stay on campus, John Z. and Jase Bagwell told me that I could stay in their rooms.

That summer was kind of amazing. Britt and Kenedy Dawson's wedding was really wonderful. At their wedding, Jace asked me to be a groomsman at his wedding the next summer. Foster was the DJ, playing all kinds of great music including "Hips Don't Lie," my walk-up song from *Who's the Man*. Another song that people ended up associating with me is Blondie's "Heart of Glass." I also worked at both Shiloh and Kanakuk camp. I could write a whole other novel about the difference between those two.

My last semester of college started the same way that my first semester of college did: with a seminar. It was a student teaching seminar. It was a week of new speakers, how to write a resume, and taking certifications like the bloodborne pathogens test so we would be qualified to get students Band-Aids. After that week, it was back to my old stomping ground of Alcott Middle School. Where I was teaching sixth-grade geography. I drove up to Bethany most every night and then back to Norman to teach. At nights on Tuesdays, I had a night class, but most other nights I was doing something fun like playing cards with the guys or being part of an improv club.

My favorite nights were the ones that I went to an SNU sporting event.

As I reflected on this, I was becoming a master of two worlds. I was slowly crossing the threshold back into the world out of college. One of the biggest memories was the first SNU football game of the season. I was chosen to go down to the field and take part in a bike race. The Stormchasers wore new uniforms for that year with the nicknames on the backs. John Z's nickname was Josh

George, because he wanted to be just like me and win my award. I heard five different people tell me that they wanted to win my award for this year. There were also five other people that told me I might win my own award again this year.

Soon, it was the 10th of November. That night SNUs men's basketball team started a major streak and tipped off a huge season beating some team from Kansas 69–55. They only lost one game between November and December of me graduating. This team's success and the attendance were so amazing. Soon, that semester had come and gone, and I had little left to accomplish at SNU. I remember lots of things that rolled around in my head just before graduation.

As I was pacing around, I just wanted to graduate. I knew I had left an impact, but had I done enough? Then I posed these questions to Baur and Leesburg. The two men that were with me. I also asked them things like, "What was the future to be like?" "How long was this graduation really going to last?" "Was there time for one last prank?"

I was standing there, about to go across the stage, about to go into the gym. The gym that Leesburg told me was my gym. As I went into the gym, I was in between Baur and Leesburg.

Ecclesiastes 3 states that there is a time for everything. So that must mean there is a time to graduate college. This was my time to graduate. I walked into that gym, and I realized it really was my time to graduate. I turned to Leesburg and made a bet not long before taking my seat. He had made me a part of the group, and I made the bet knowing that one day we would indeed have to see each other once more. It was not long until a man took the stage to give the commencement speech. He started talking about all the good deeds we had done and would go on to do, but as he started to close, he stated a quote. This quote was a major theme in my college career.

As he started into the quote, Baur and I started saying it also. We said, "You cannot connect the dots looking forward. You can only connect the dots looking backward, so you have to trust that the dots will somehow connect in your future. You have to trust in something: Your gut, destiny, life, whatever. Because that will give you the courage to follow your heart even when it leads you off the well-worn path." These words would give me the confidence to go on no matter what, and the point of this book is to help you find ways to persevere no matter what.

Other things to note: I won the bet. I walked across the stage and got my diploma. There were photos taken at the entrance to the gym. These photos were taken in front of a glass case that displayed my award. The award in my namesake, the Josh George Award. It was to be given out to the best fan of SNU athletics. I had started something great. I was pleased, but I did not know that it would end this way, nor did I ever think of getting honored like this.

I still did not think that my journey was over.

I ended up substituting in a school district in parts of Oklahoma City and spending some nights on Jase's couch. I got to be a part of SNU winning back-to-back conference titles in men's basketball and other titles in other sports. In an incredible season, SNU ended up winning the conference title, and during the conference championship, I wound up with a group of children behind the basket. I taught them a little about what I knew. I felt like SNU would have a fresh set of storm chasers for the days to come, a fresh set of Josh Georges for the future. If it was not at that moment that I felt the freedom to live, then it was when I gave out the award in my namesake to the second winner, Andrew Marstin. I remember that night very vividly. There were three finalists, and they all told me how thrilled that they would be to win this award. It let me know that I had left SNU in good hands. I still go to a game from time to time, but I usually sit far away from the action, and sometimes I watch the student section more than I do the actual game. One last thing to remember: you are you, so be who you are.

The End!

As I reflect on my college experience, I think about the big things like the award and the record on the disc golf course, but it is all the little moments that make up a college career. The little moments like running into some unsuspecting guys' room dressed as close to the Village People and randomly dancing. Having some of your close friends dress up in weird costumes to help you ask a girl to a dance. There are also many lessons of perseverance, like overcoming the moment a girl rejects you after first agreeing to go out with you. College can be a real rage, and I had a great time. If there's some last bit of advice for you, it would probably be this: go to class. I know that I rarely mentioned class in this book, but it is a very essential reason of college, and I never skipped class for any of my adventures and only missed class three times: one time I overslept; the other was when I spent too long in the library and forgot about my afternoon class; and the other was to go to a funeral. So, go to class, then use the free time you have to be creative and have fun and find ways to make an impact on your school.

With this, sometimes a legacy is much more than a record or an award. Most legacies are the people that you impact. There is a moment that sticks out in my mind that took place after an SNU football game.

There was no OU game, so my parents went to see me lead the students' section at SNU, and after the game we went out to eat at Louie's. As we were leaving, a football player and his parents both said hi to me and knew me by name, and his dad was the one that flagged me down to be sure and say hi and meet my family. Earlier this year, I was part of a Zoom meeting with some of the guys from college and their spouses. Some of whom went to college with us, and it was great because of how great the bond is. We enjoyed reconnecting playing online games and talking about old memories as well as the difficulties of life now. So, if you want to know if you had an impact on your college or left a legacy, wait years, then talk to your old friends and you'll know. If you want to know how to leave a legacy, it is simple: do your best to make connections with people on your campus. This happens by asking people to help you with your endeavors as well as being willing to help others with what they need.

Love God and love others; it really is that simple. Without this and the people I was around, there would be no Josh George award.

The real end!